NAVIGATOR'S NOTEBOOK

NAVIGATOR'S NOTEBOOK:

A Workbook for Marine Navigation

Anthony Palmiotti

CORNELL MARITIME PRESS

A Division of Schiffer Publishing, Ltd.

Atglen, Pennsylvania

DEDICATION

This book is dedicated to Captain Harry Fleureton. In a world filled with phonies and wanna-bees, Captain Harry was the real deal. He was a consummate seaman and a true friend.

Cover Designed by Bruce Waters
Designed by Matt Goodman
Type set in Trade Gothic and Clarendon

ISBN: 978-0-87033-630-0
Printed in The United States of America

Published by Schiffer Publishing, Ltd.
4880 Lower Valley Road
Atglen, PA 19310
Phone: (610) 593-1777; Fax: (610) 593-2002
E-mail: Info@schifferbooks.com

For our complete selection of fine books on this and related subjects, please visit our website at www.schifferbooks.com. You may also write for a free catalog.

This book may be purchased from the publisher. Please try your bookstore first.

We are always looking for people to write books on new and related subjects. If you have an idea for a book, please contact us at proposals@schifferbooks.com

Schiffer Publishing's titles are available at special discounts for bulk purchases for sales promotions or premiums. Special editions, including personalized covers, corporate imprints, and excerpts can be created in large quantities for special needs. For more information, contact the publisher.

CONTENTS

INTRODUCTION

It's a common practice for professional mariners to carry with them a navigational notebook. In this notebook are examples of problems, formulas, and memory aids that make life in the pilothouse a little easier and help with the many calculations that are required for careful and accurate navigation. This reference is like that notebook.

Included here are formulas and examples of common navigational problems that the ocean and coastal navigator may have to use. This is not a "how to" text, it is intended to jog the memory and give a quick example of the most common problems used in the practice of navigation. Like anything, there is more than one way to solve some of these problems. The methods used here are the result of many years of seafaring and teaching and have been successful both in practice and in preparation for a Coast Guard license.

When referring to this book feel free to make your own notes and memory aids so that next time you're faced with the same problem the solution is at your fingertips.

CHAPTER ONE

CALCULATIONS IN TERRESTRIAL NAVIGATION

"Why is almost every robust, healthy boy with a robust, healthy soul in him, at some time or other, crazy to go to sea?"

—Herman Melville, Moby Dick

BASIC DEFINITIONS IN TERRESTRIAL NAVIGATION

Directional: Many times there is a difference between the direction the vessel is pointing and the direction it is actually traveling. Understand the differences in the definitions below.

Heading: Generally considered the compass course of the vessel; the direction in which the vessel is pointing. Heading is stated in degrees, 0° – 360°, and should agree with the compass being used. The difference between compass heading and true heading is discussed in the section on compasses. A vessel's heading may be different on different compasses given the compass error inherent in each individual compass.

Heading is the direction the vessel is pointing based on the compass course.

Course Made Good/ Course over the Ground: Environmental factors such as wind and current may push a vessel away from its heading and cause its actual track over the earth to be different from the direction it is pointing.

The actual track of a vessel over the ground is the course made good. Take a look at the figure on page 8 (01-01), although the vessel is heading in one direction, compass course of 045°, the effect of the wind, or current, is to give a course over the ground to the left.

Course made good is to the left of the heading

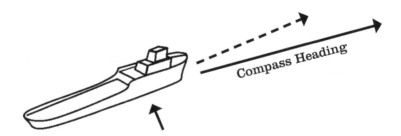

East Wind Pushes Vessel to the Left Creating **Leeway**

Course to Steer: This is the compass course needed to "make good" the true or desired course. This is the course to steer to counter the effects of wind or current. In the diagram on page 8, the vessel should steer to the right of its compass course to make good the course it wants. When the vessel is affected by current it is called set and drift. When the vessel is affected by wind it is called leeway.

Bearing: A bearing indicates the direction to an object from your position. Bearings can be stated as true or relative.

True Bearings: True bearings use true north as the basis for direction. The beauty of true bearings is that they can be plotted directly onto a nautical chart. On a vessel underway bearings are usually taken using a gyro repeater or from the radar, which has gyro input. If the gyro compass has error, then the error must be accounted for before plotting.

Relative Bearings: Relative uses the ship's bow as the reference point and then measures clockwise through 360°.

A vessel is heading 045° true. The vessel abeam to starboard is bearing 135° true or 090° relative

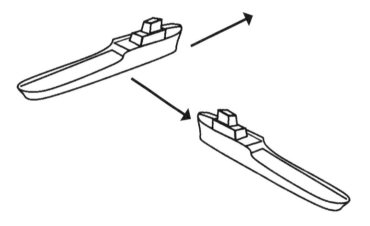

Definitions for Distance and Length

Cable: One tenth of a nautical mile, 607.6 feet. In the old days, the length of a standard anchor chain.

Fathom: 6 feet

Meter: 3.28 feet

Nautical mile: 6,076 feet. One minute of arc at the equator or on any great circle is considered to equal one nautical mile.

Statute mile: 5,280 feet

Shot: One shot of anchor chain is 90 feet or 15 fathoms

Definitions for Speed

Knot: one nautical mile per hour

Speed made good: Speed of the vessel determined from calculation between fixes.

Speed over the ground: This is the actual speed of the vessel over the surface of the earth.

Speed through the water: This is the speed the vessel is making as it passes through the water. For example, a vessel turning for 10 kts. with a 2 kt. following current would have a speed of 10 kts. through the water but 12 kts. over the ground. Similarly, a vessel whose engines are not turning may have no way through the water but still have speed over the ground equal to the speed of the current.

In the figure on page XX (01-03), the vessel is making turns for 10 kts, the current is moving at 2 kts. The speed through the water is 10 kts. But the speed over the ground is 12 kts.

A following current increases speed over the ground

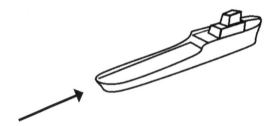

Current is 2 kts. + Vessel turning at 10kts.
= Speed over the ground 12 kts.

Position: The art of navigation isn't just about where the vessel is, but, just as important, where the vessel is heading. Being able to project the future track of the vessel is critical to staying out of trouble. There are very definite differences between the positioning definitions below.

Fix: You have "fixed" the vessels position when you can plot a position on a chart that is independent of other fixes. For example, a good set of terrestrial bearings, a good electronic position, or a solid radar range and bearing. A fix is shown on the chart as a dot surrounded by a circle. ◉

Dead Reckoning Position (DR): A DR position is when you project your position into the future based on a known position. It is where you think you will be based on speed and heading. A DR position is shown as a half circle with a dot. The figure on page XX is a 0800 fix, DR'ed out to 1200. Speed is 10 kts, so the distance between DR's is 10 miles.

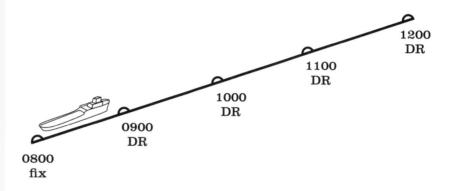

Estimated Position: An estimated position is a refined dead reckoning position. An estimated position not only considers speed and heading but wind and/or current. Using the DR positions above, if we knew there was a current setting us to the north our estimated 1200 position would be indicated by the square with a dot in the center and our actual track would have been the dotted line.

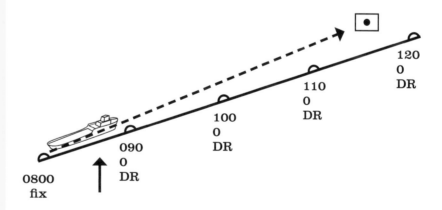

MEASUREMENT ON THE EARTH —LATITUDE AND LONGITUDE

Being able to determine the difference of Latitude and difference of Longitude is critical to many navigational calculations. Since these measures are base 60, not base 10, they can't be directly done using a calculator unless the minutes are turned into a decimal (minutes/60). For example, 25°- 30' is the same as 25.5°.

Longitude is measured East and West of the Prime Meridian (Greenwich Meridian) through 180° in both directions. At the equator one minute of arc equals one nautical mile. Distance between lines of longitude decreases to zero as lines reach the poles. A line of Longitude may also be known as a meridian.

North

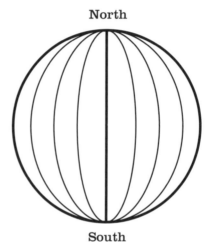

South

Latitude is measured north and south of the equator through 90°. All lines of latitude are parallel to each other. The equator is considered a Great Circle; all other lines of latitude are considered Small Circles.

North

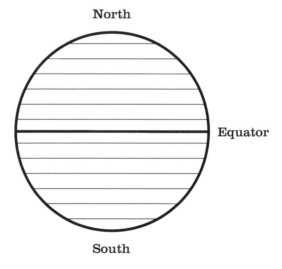

Equator

South

Calculating Difference of Longitude and Difference of Latitude

Examples: Difference of Longitude

1. **Same Longitude (both east or both west):** Same longitude, subtract smaller from larger: **A vessel is sailing from longitude 157°- 35 East to 124°- 20 East. What is the difference of longitude (DLO)?**

$$
\begin{array}{rl}
& 157° \;\text{-}35\text{E} \\
+ & 124° \;\text{-}20\text{E} \\
\hline
\text{DLO} = & 33° \;\text{-}15
\end{array}
$$

2. **Different Longitude:** Going from one longitude (east or west) to another and passing through O° then add east and west longitude together: **A vessel is sailing from longitude 37°-55 East to 42°- 23 West through the Greenwich meridian (0°). What is the difference of Longitude?**

$$
\begin{array}{rl}
& 37° \;\text{-}55\text{E} \\
+ & 42° \;\text{-}23\text{W} \\
\hline
\text{DLO} = & 80° \;\text{-}18
\end{array}
$$

3. **Different Longitude:** If passing through 180° (179°- 60) then subtract both east and west longitude from 180° and then add the two results together: **A vessel is sailing from 175° - 33 East to 165°-24 West through 180°. What is the difference of longitude?**

Subtract Long.	from 180°	Add differences
179° -60	179° -60	14° -36
-175° -33	-165° -24	+ 4° -27
4° -27	14° -36	DLO= 19° -03

Examples: Difference of Latitude

1. When staying in the same hemisphere, subtract the smaller from the larger: **A vessel is sailing from 36°- 40 N to 15°- 26 N. What is the difference of Latitude?**

$$
\begin{array}{rl}
& 36° \;\text{-}40\text{N} \\
- & 15° \;\text{-}26\text{N} \\
\hline
\text{Dlat} = & 21° \;\text{-}14
\end{array}
$$

2. When going from one hemisphere to another, (i.e., crossing the equator) add north and south: A vessel is sailing from 36°- 40 N to 15°- 26 S. What is the difference of Latitude?

	36°	-40N
	+15°	-26S
Dlat=	52°	-06

A QUICK OVERVIEW OF TIME AND TIME ZONES

In the practice of navigation, as in life, certain assumptions are made to make the process easier. For example, in celestial navigation it is assumed that the earth is the center of the universe and the sun, planets, and stars circle around it on a celestial sphere. More about the celestial sphere later; here it is important to picture the sun circling the earth at a constant rate and the earth as a perfect sphere of 360°. It is also assumed that every day has exactly 24 hours. Given these assumptions, the sun moves around the earth at a rate of 15 degrees per hour (360°/24 hrs = 15 °/hr).

Time Zones were developed to keep a certain order in how we all keep time. Since the sun moves constantly its necessary to standardize time geographically to keep everyone from having a different time as the sun marched ceaselessly across the sky.

Time Zones, like longitude, start at the Greenwich Meridian, which is considered Greenwich Mean Time (GMT or Universal Time). Greenwich is O° longitude and the Greenwich time zone is measured 7 1/2° on either side of zero, giving the 15° time zone for GMT. Every time zone is measured 7 1/2° on either side of the central meridian. For example, the time zone at ZD +2, 30° west, measures from 22 1/2° West to 37 1/2° West.

Central Meridians are measured every 15° east and west of the Greenwich meridian. Since the sun appears to travel east to west in the sky, West longitude is considered plus (+) and East longitude is considered minus (-). Central meridians are shown in the table below:

Central Meridians

0°	15°	30°	45°	60°	75°	90°	105°	120°	135°	150°	165°	180°
0	-/+1	-/+2	-/+3	-/+4	-/+5	-/+6	-/+7	-/+8	-/+9	-/+10	-/+11	-/+12

Zone Description East-/West+(ZD)

Meridians in East longitude are labeled – because it is necessary to subtract the zone description to determine the time at GMT from an east longitude location.

Meridians in West longitude are labeled + because it is necessary to add the zone description to determine the time at GMT from a west longitude location.

Examples   **If New York City is in ZD +5 and it is 1000 in New York, what time is it GMT?**

$$
\begin{array}{l}
1000 \\
\underline{+\ 5} \\
1500 \quad \textbf{GMT}
\end{array}
$$

If Istanbul, Turkey, is in ZD -2 and it is 1000 in Istanbul, what time is it GMT?

$$
\begin{array}{l}
1000 \\
\underline{-\ 2} \\
0800 \quad \textbf{GMT}
\end{array}
$$

If Istanbul, Turkey, is in ZD -2 and it is 1000 in Istanbul, and New York City is in ZD +5. What time is it in New York? Going from east to west subtract time (the sun hasn't reached NY yet)

$$
\begin{array}{l}
1000 \\
\underline{-\ 7} \\
0300 \quad \textbf{New York Time}
\end{array}
$$

Zone Description

Being able to determine zone description is an important component of many celestial navigation and estimated time of arrival (ETA) problems. To determine zone description divide the longitude by 15.

For fractions: If the decimal is less than 0.5 than you are in the time zone represented by the whole number.

If the decimal is over 0.5 you would round up to the next whole number.

Example   What is the zone description of:

Long 95° -36°E = 95.6°, 95.6° /15 = 6.37
zone description = -6

Long 98° -36°E = 98.6°, 98.6° /15 = 6.57
zone description = -7

The border for the – 6 zone description would be 97°- 30'. Once your vessel passes the border you are considered to be in the next time zone.

SPEED AND TIME CALCULATIONS

There are two basic types of speed and time problems. The first kind asks when we are going to get there; estimated time of arrival (ETA) problems. The second kind of problem requires what speed is necessary to get to a certain point at a specified time; the speed to make good a time of arrival. Being able to accurately predict arrival time, or determine the speed needed to make good arrival at a particular time is a very important skill for the mariner.

Estimated Time of Arrival (ETA)

ETA problems assume a constant speed over a given distance. The result is the time it is going to take to go that distance. Very rarely is the speed of a vessel constant. Always remember that an ETA is just that, an estimated time of arrival. ETA problems use the formula:

Distance = Speed x Time

Or, solving for Time

Time = Distance / Speed

Note

Speed at sea is never constant and is always subject to wind, current, and sea condition. Although a ship's speed may be estimated by the number of revolutions of the propeller, sea conditions always affect the vessel's actual speed made good. The further away the vessel is from the destination, the less accurate the ETA is going to be. ETA's should be refined regularly with up to date speed over the ground information.

Example 1

A vessel has 65 miles to go to reach the sea buoy. Assuming an average speed over the ground of 15 knots:

1. How long will the trip take?

> **Time= 65 nautical miles / 15 nmph = 4.33 hours
> or 4 hours and 20 minutes (.33 x 60 min. = 20 min.)**

Note   Units must be the same, i.e., hours and miles per hour result in an answer in hours (4.33). Mixed units give the wrong answer.

2. What time will the vessel arrive at the destination if the time now is 1220?

```
  12 -20
 + 4 -20
  16 -40  ETA
```

3. If the distance remains the same, 65 nautical miles, and speed is decreased to 10 knots, what is the ETA? Time= 65/ 10= 6.5 hours or 6 hours, 30 minutes. Then the ETA is:

```
  12 -20
 + 6 -30
  18 -50  ETA
```

▶ ## Speed to Make Good a Time of Arrival

Many times it's necessary to work from a certain time. It may be necessary to time an arrival for a certain state of tide, to make a pilot time, etc. For this calculation, simply solve for speed.

▶ ## Speed necessary given fixed time and distance

Speed= Distance / time

1. Distance to the pilot station is 245 nm, it is now Tuesday at 1630. What is the speed needed to arrive at the pilot station at 0600 on Wednesday.

Difference of Time:
Wednesday 0600- from Tuesday 1630
= 13 hrs 30 min or 13.5 hrs
Speed= 245 nm/ 13.5 hrs= 18.15 knots

2. You wish to arrive at a particular point at slack water. The distance to the area is 78 miles and slack water is at 1645. The time now is 0910. What is the speed required?

Difference of Time:
0910 to 1645 = 7 hours 35 min or 8.58 hrs.
Speed = 78 nm/ 7.58 hrs = 10.29 kts

▶ ## ETA Across Time Zones

Sometimes it's necessary to estimate times of arrival well in advance from departure at one port until arrival at the next. Obviously, the longer the distance, the less accurate since speeds at sea are always subject to factors such as weather and currents. Despite this, ETA's are important for planning port services and other ship support functions. Below is an example of an ETA across multiple time zones:

Process

1. Take the time of departure and convert to Greenwich Mean Time (GMT).

2. Calculate time to run using speed/time/distance formula and add this to the GMT time.

3. Convert GMT to local time of arrival at destination

Example

At 0915 zone time, on 7 November, you depart Seattle, LAT 47°36.0'N, LONG 122°22.0'W (ZD +8). You are bound for Kobe, Japan, LAT 34°40.0'N, LONG 135°12.0'E, (ZD -9) and you estimate your speed of advance at 18.5 knots. The distance is 4,527 miles. What is your estimated zone time of arrival at Kobe?

1. Take the time of departure and convert to Greenwich Mean Time (GMT).

Seattle-	0915	7 Nov.
ZD	+ 8	
GMT	1715	7 Nov

2. Calculate time to run using speed/time/distance formula

4527 miles/ 18.5 knots= 244.7 hours
244.7 hours/ 24 hrs/day= 10.196 days
.196 day x 24 hours= 4.7 hours
.7 x 60 minutes= 42 minutes

GMT	17 -15	7 Nov,
	+4 -42	10
GMT	21 -57	17 Nov. (arrival time at GMT)

3. Convert GMT to local time of arrival, 9 hours to Kobe

GMT	2157	17 Nov.
ZD	+9	
L. T.	0657	18 November, Local Time in Kobe, Japan

Note

Add 9 hours going from GMT to Kobe, Japan, since it is in East Longitude.

SET AND DRIFT

Environmental factors such as current and wind affect the track of a vessel. When a vessel is pushed off its course by current it is called Set (direction) and Drift (speed of current). When the vessel is affected by wind, it is called Leeway. Vessels that have a lot of freeboard or "sail area" are affected by the wind to a greater extent than those that are low in the water. There is no magic formula for predicting how a vessel will be influenced by the wind. The course to steer to make good the course desired is found by monitoring the vessel's position and through experience.

Set and Drift problems can be worked out on a paper chart or on a maneuvering board. The objective is to create a vector triangle where two sides are known and the third is solved.

Process

1. Draw a line representing vessel's course and speed. This can be for one hour or any part of an hour but if the vector is drawn for less than an hour, then all other vectors must/will represent the same time frame.

2. Draw a line representing the set (direction) and drift (speed) of the current and connect to the end of the course line.

3. The resultant is the course made good and the length of the line represents speed made good over the time measured.

Note

If the navigator knows 1 above, course and speed, and takes a fix to determine the course made good, 2, then it is possible to calculate the set and drift of the current.

Course Made Good

A vessel is on course 090° T at a speed of 10 knots and a current of 135° (set) is 2 knots (drift). What is the course made good?

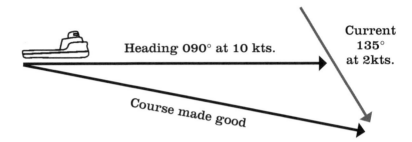

The actual track of the vessel is along the resultant line. This is the course made good.

Course to Steer to Make Good a True Course

A vessel wants to make good a course of 090° T. There is a 2 kt. current at 135° T. What is the Course to Steer to make good the desired course, 090° T?

To maintain a course over the ground of 090° T, it is necessary to steer into the current to counter the effects of the current. The resultant line is the course to steer given current direction, set, and speed, drift.

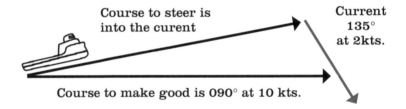

LEEWAY

Just as a vessel's course and speed over the ground can be affected by current, it can also be affected by wind. When a vessel is pushed off its heading by the wind it is called making Leeway.

Wind is always labeled from the direction it is coming so an East wind is coming from the east and pushing a vessel in a westerly direction. A South wind is from the south and pushing the vessel in a northerly direction.

Example

1. A vessel is heading 090° T and a south wind produces 3° of Leeway. What is the course made good?

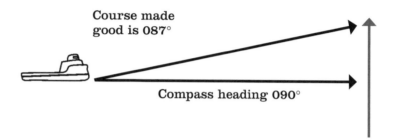

Course made good is 087°

Compass heading 090°

2. A vessel is heading 090° T and a south wind produces 3° of Leeway. What is the course to steer to make good the desired course?

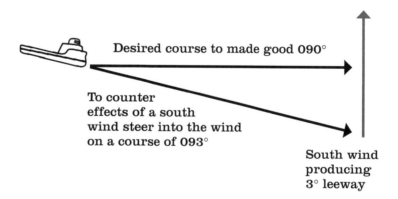

Desired course to made good 090°

To counter effects of a south wind steer into the wind on a course of 093°

South wind producing 3° leeway

CHAPTER TWO
COMPASSES & COMPASS ERROR

"No matter how important a man at sea may
consider himself, unless he is fundamentally worthy
the sea will someday find him out."

Felix Riesenberg

There are two types of compasses found onboard most commercial vessels, the old stand-by magnetic compass and the gyro compass. The gyro compass requires electrical power to operate while the magnetic does not. The good, old magnetic compass works even if all other systems are down. When passage planning, courses should always be computed for both a gyro course and a magnetic compass course so steering can be "checked" in the event of an electrical failure.

The magnetic compass is both the simplest and the most misunderstood instrument onboard. Used correctly it can take you accurately through foggy mornings and across oceans. Used without understanding of its basic principles and faults, the compass can lead both the ship and crew into danger.

Every compass should be checked for accuracy regularly, once a watch on a commercial ship. When in piloting waters, a compass can be checked against a known navigational range. When the vessel is at sea, the compass should be checked by taking either an azimuth or amplitude of a celestial body when the opportunity arises.

Remember, the true course plotted on a chart will only match the course to be steered if it has been determined that there is no error in the compass.

COMPASS DEFINITIONS

Magnetic Compass: A magnetic compass is a compass that relies on the earth's magnetic field to indicate north. Because the magnetic north pole and the geographic North Pole are not in the same location, there is an inherent error in every magnetic compass. This error is called **Variation** (see below). Magnetic compasses are also subject to the magnetic field that surrounds every ship, this error is called **Deviation** (see below). On larger ships, the magnetic compass is not normally the primary method of determining direction, but is used as a back-up to the Gyro compass. The magnetic compass on many large vessels is located on the flying bridge to avoid as much ship-based magnetic influence as possible and is seen visually in the pilot house using mirrors in a special periscope. When courses are given using the magnetic compass, they are referred to as Per Standard Compass (PSC) course.

Gyro Compass: A gyro compass is an electrically driven compass that relies on the principle of a north seeking gyro, not unlike a spinning top. A benefit of the gyro compass is that it may be connected to one or more gyro-repeaters located throughout the vessel. The gyro compass is not only the primary compass onboard a large vessel but its data is fed to other equipment such as the radar and ECDIS, making its reliability and accuracy critical for safe navigation. Because of its electrical requirements and weight, it is not generally found on smaller recreational vessels.

Gyro compasses are not subject to magnetic variation or ship-based deviation as are magnetic compasses, but may have their own inherent Gyro Error.

True Course: That heading with reference to geographic North and without the influence of any kind of compass error (i.e., either variation or deviation or gyro error). Course lines and bearings drawn on a chart should always be shown as True courses. On the compass rose of a paper chart True is the outer circle.

Magnetic course: That heading with reference to the magnetic pole. The difference between Magnetic North and True North is the Variation in the geographic area. This is the course shown on a magnetic compass if there was no ship-based deviation. On the compass rose of a paper chart magnetic headings are shown on the inner circle.

Variation: That error in a magnetic compass that is the result of the earth's magnetic field. Variation changes with position on the earth. Lines of equal variation are called isogonic lines. Variation for any locality can be found in the compass rose on a chart or as isogonic lines on a pilot chart. Variation also changes, even if only slightly, every year as the magnetic poles shift their location.

Compass Course: That course shown on a magnetic compass after the effects of Variation and Deviation. The compass course can be calculated from the true course by applying the known variation in the area and the deviation for that magnetic heading.

> **True +/- Variation =**
> **Magnetic Heading +/- Deviation =**
> **Compass Course**

Deviation: That error inherent in the compass that is the effect of the ship's magnetic influences. Deviation is recorded on a deviation card and is different on different headings but the same for any geographic location. **Remember:** Deviation differs on different headings. Variation differs in different geographic locations

Gyro Error: Gyro compasses are not subject to variation or deviation but most Gyro compasses have an inherent error. The difference between the gyro compass heading and true heading is called Gyro Error. The amount of the error is the same for any heading, any location.

Compass Error: The cumulative effect of all error in a compass between true and compass heading. In a magnetic compass, this would be the combination of deviation and variation. In a gyro compass, this would be gyro error.

Swinging Ship: Every vessel should check the deviation in its magnetic compass annually or after any major work has been done that may change the vessel's magnetic signature. The process by which the compass is checked against known bearings and a deviation table made is called swinging ship.

Deviation Table: A table or chart usually posted on the wall of the pilothouse that shows what the deviation is on different magnetic headings.

See Appendix 3
for Swing Ship and Deviation Table Worksheets

CALCULATING COMPASS ERROR

Over a short distance, when there are other visual references to help determine the vessel's position, a few degrees of compass error can be compensated for by observation and maintaining a good plot on a chart or using other tools to monitor position, such as GPS. However, when the vessel is headed over the horizon or in times of limited visibility it is critical that the navigator apply the correct compass error.

Courses plotted on a chart are always drawn as True courses. To determine the course to steer per magnetic compass, it is necessary to add or subtract the variation to get the magnetic heading and then add or subtract the deviation to get the compass course.

Calculating Magnetic Compass Error

True Course +/- Variation =
Magnetic Course +/- Deviation =
Compass Course

1. Going from True to Compass add west error and subtract east error

2. Going from Compass to True add east error and subtract west error

CALCULATING GYRO COMPASS ERROR

Gyro Course +/- Error= True Course

Rules When going from Gyro Course to True Course Add East error and Subtract West error.

When going from True Course to Gyro Course Add West error and Subtract East error.

Examples 1. Your destination is on a true heading of 110°, Variation in the area is 3.5 west, and Deviation is 5.0 east. **What compass course should we steer? What is the compass error?**

T	V	M	D	C
110°	3.5W	113.5°	5.0E	108.5°

Compass Error: 1.5 East (110 – 108.5)

2. A vessel is steering a compass course (psc) of 270°. If variation is 4.0 west and deviation on this heading 2.5 west, what is the true course? What is the compass error?

T	V	M	D	C
263.5°	4.0W	267.5°	2.5W	270°

Compass Error: 6.5 West

3. Gyro Course is 334° and gyro error is 1.5 west. What is the true course?

Gyro	Error	True
334°	1.5W	332.5°

COMPASS CORRECTION AT SEA—AZIMUTH OR AMPLITUDE

What these accomplish

At sea, when there are no terrestrial features to take bearings of, it is possible to take a bearing of a known celestial body, such as the sun, and, knowing the exact time and the ship's location, check the accuracy of the compass by calculating the true bearing of the celestial body. This is known as an Azimuth. Using the Nautical Almanac and HO 229, it is possible to determine the azimuth (bearing) to the body and compare it with the observed bearing to get the compass error.

Another method of checking the compass at sea is the Amplitude. An amplitude is taken only during rising or setting, when the sun is at or near the horizon. An Azimuth is taken when the body is higher in altitude, usually twenty degrees or more.

Method

An Azimuth or an Amplitude is taken using an azimuth circle on either a gyro repeater or magnetic compass. The celestial body is "sighted" for a bearing and the exact time noted.

Azimuths

Information needed when working out an azimuth:

- **Exact time of sight, (hour, minute, second) brought to Greenwich Mean Time (GMT)**
- **Bearing to celestial body taken over compass to be checked.**
- **The Latitude and Longitude at the time of the bearing**

Method to calculate an Azimuth

Definitions for the terms below can be found in the section describing sight reduction. To calculate an azimuth or amplitude requires the navigator to be familiar with the Nautical Almanac, publication H.O. 229 and to have knowledge of how these publications are used in sight reduction. The terms below are defined in the section on sight reduction.

Local Hour Angle (LHA) of Body
(LHA = Greenwich Hour Angle - West / + East Longitude)
Declination
Latitude

Step 1

Using the Nautical Almanac for the current year, calculate the LHA of the Body and the declination at the time of the sight using the GMT for the time of the sight. LHA is calculated by looking up the GHA of the body at the time of the bearing and then either adding or subtracting longitude:

GHA (hrs)   Declination:
Cor. (mins/sec) _____   +/-d _____
GHA of Body   Declination
Longitude
(- west/+ east) _____
LHA of Body

Example of Step 1

On February 18th your vessel is in latitude 23°-17.8 N and longitude 013°- 58.4 W when an azimuth of the sun is taken. Time is 09hrs-42min-09 sec GMT. Find the declination of the sun and LHA at that time.

1. Go to Nautical Almanac for February 18th and find GHA and declination for time of sight (see Appendix 4).

2. In the Nautical Almanac go to Increments and Corrections pages for minutes/seconds and d correction. Add minutes and seconds to hourly GHA and either add or subtract d correction as appropriate

3. Find LHA by subtracting (-) west longitude and adding (+) east longitude

See Appendix 4
Nautical Almanac for GHA and Declination

GHA (09 hrs)	311° -30.3	Declination:	S 11° -36.2 (d= .9)
(42 mins/ 09 sec)	10° -32.3	d Corr	0.6
GHA of Body	322° -02.6	Declination	S 11° -35.6
Longitude (- west,+ east)	-013° -58.4		
LHA of Body	308° -04.2		

Step 2

With the LHA, declination and the closest whole latitude to your location enter the HO 229 **as shown in Appendix 4** and get the azimuth angle, Z. What needs to happen for accuracy is a three-way interpolation to account for minutes of LHA, Latitude and declination. The table below shows a simple way to account for all three.

Example

Using the following inputs: A bearing was taken from the gyro compass, 126.5 pgc. After calculation of LHA and declination from the nautical almanac we have the following data:

LHA- 308°-04.2   Lat.-23°-17.8N   Declination- 11°-36.5 S

Actual (from HO 229)	Base Argument	Base Z	Tabular Z	Z Diff	Increments from Actual	Correction Z Diff x Increm/60
LHA 308°-04.2	308	118	118.7	0.7	4.2	0.05
Lat 23°-17.8N	23	118	118.5	0.5	17.8	0.15
Dec 11°-35.6S	11	118	129	1.0	35.6	0.59
					Total Correction	0.79 Round to 0.8

Step by Step Explanation

1. Determine Base Arguments by using the whole number of LHA, Lat, Dec.

2. Using Base Arguments enter HO 229 and go to the proper page using LHA, Lat, and Dec. Remember to check if Lat and Dec are in the same or different hemisphere (i.e., N lat and N Dec) and take Z from the appropriate page. In this case, the Base Z is 118. This is found by going to HO 229, Vol 2 and looking for the inputs LHA 308, Lat 23, Dec 11.

Latitude is the same as declination, so look in the left hand page of the HO 229 (Appendix 4).

3. Tabular Z is the Z in the next higher entry for each base argument.

For example, in this case with an LHA of 308 look for 309 with Lat remaining at 23 and Dec. at 11. In this case, for tabular Z use Lat of 24 and LHA 309, Dec. 12.

4. Calculate the difference between tabular Z and base to determine the Z Difference. Be aware of signs, negative or positive.

5. Take increments (minutes) from actual inputs. **Note:** for LHA of 318-04.2 it would be 04.2.

6. Apply the formula:

Z diff x (Inc /60).
Dec- 0.8 x (4.2 / 60) = 0.05

Apply this formula for each input and get the sum. This is the correction for base Z:

Base Z	118.0°
Cor.	0.8
Z	118.8°
Zn (true)	118.8°
ZN Obs	121.5 pgc
Gyro Error	2.7 E

Another Method -By Formula

If the table above is too confusing, or you have a scientific calculator, the true Z can be found from the following formula:

$$\text{Tan Z} = \frac{\cos d \times \sin \text{LHA}}{(\cos L \sin d) - (\sin L \cos d \cos \text{LHA})}$$

Where d= declination
L= latitude
LHA= LHA

Note

1. If LHA is greater than 180 than subtract answer from 180.

2. If Latitude and declination are contrary (i.e., North latitude and South Declination) then Sin d, in the denominator, is negative.

Using the same declination, latitude, and LHA from above:

$$\text{Tan Z} = \frac{\cos 11.59° \ \text{x} \ \sin 308.07°}{(\cos 23.3°\text{x -sin } 11.59°) - (\sin 23.3°\text{x cos } 11.59°\text{x cos } 08.07°°)}$$

Tan Z= 1.82135

Z= 180- 61.2= 118.8°

The answer gotten by calculation may be slightly different than the tables due to rounding.

Amplitude: Amplitudes are taken when the celestial body is either on the celestial horizon or the visible horizon.

Visible Horizon- the line where the earth and sea meet.

Celestial Horizon- for amplitudes of the sun, it is considered to be on the celestial horizon when the lower limb is a little more than half a diameter above the visible horizon.

 The actual true bearing is derived by either adding or subtracting from East or West (90° or 270°) using the rules below.

Prefix/suffix: Prefix- E is for rising, W is for setting. Suffix- N or S to agree with the declination of the body.

Example   **E 1.5 N = 88.5 degrees (90° – 1.5= 88.5°)**

      W 1.0 S = 269 degrees (270° – 1= 269°)

To Calculate an Amplitude

A bearing of the sun is taken at sunrise or sunset, when it is just touching the horizon (visible horizon) or about half a diameter above it (celestial horizon). The exact time down to the second is noted along with the latitude at the time of the sight.

Step 1: Enter the Nautical Almanac and get the Declination of the body at the time of the sight.

Step 2: Enter the Amplitudes table found in the back of Bowditch and find tabulated value for Latitude and Declination.

Example An amplitude at Sunset taken at, Lat- 51- 24.6 N, Dec. N 19°-40.4.

Source: Amplitudes table in Bowditch

	Declination		
Latitude	19.5°		20.0°
51°	31.2		32.0
Interpolate	31.9°	32.6°	32.7°
52°	32.8°		33.7°

Using Prefix for sunset (W) and Latitude (N)

W 32.6 N or 302.6 ° (270° + 32.6°= 302.6°)

Step 3   Compare Observed to calculated bearing.

Observed bearing = 303° pgc

Obs. PGC	Calc. (T)	Gyro Error
303	302.6	0.4W

Step 4   If the sight was taken on the Visible horizon, apply correction to observed bearing from table, Azimuth Observed on the Visible Horizon in Bowditch.

The amplitude can also be calculated using the formula below.

Sin Amplitude= Sin Declination/Cos Latitude

Once the amplitude is found, then the proper prefix and suffix, see above, must be applied to get the true bearing.

CHAPTER THREE
TIDES & TIDAL CURRENTS

"There is nothing more enticing, disenchanting,
and enslaving than the life at sea."
—Joseph Conrad

Tides and tidal currents are caused by a complicated dynamic of many forces: the gravitational pull of the moon and sun, as well as the spinning of the earth on its axis. As these forces interact, they have the effect of keeping the 70% of the earth's surface covered by water in constant motion. Complicating these global forces are the influence of local winds and weather, and the local geography. The overall effect is a dynamic that provides a diverse range of local tidal conditions. For example, the Mediterranean has little in the way of tidal action when compared to Maine, Nova Scotia, or Northern Europe where tidal ranges of twelve feet or more each day are common. The East Coast of the United States experiences mostly semi-diurnal tides, the Gulf Coast diurnal tides, and the West Coast mixed tides.

Tide is considered to be the vertical motion of the ocean surface, rising or falling. **Tidal currents** are considered the horizontal motion of the water, an in-flowing flood current or an out-flowing-ebb current.

A word of caution, tidal predictions should never be considered gospel, but only guidelines. Local weather conditions or shifting bottoms may make the depth of the water different from predicted or that shown on the chart. Always use caution when operating with slim under keel clearances.

DEFINITIONS

Tide Definitions

Sounding: The depth of the water indicated on a chart. On the East Coast, most NOAA charts show depths of water at Mean Lower Low Water (MLLW). Charts indicate the date of the last survey. Navigators should use caution when the survey date is old, especially in areas with sandy or soft bottoms that may shift due to weather or the actions of currents.

Height of Tide: The Tide tables indicate the height of the water above or below the soundings indicated on the chart for a specific time and day. The number calculated in the table is added (or subtracted) to the depth of water shown on the chart.

High Water: Otherwise known as High Tide, this is the time the height of tide is at its greatest in any tidal cycle.

Low Water: Otherwise known as Low Tide, this is the time the height of tide is at its lowest point in any tidal cycle.

Semi-diurnal tides: Two high and two low tides each day. On the East Coast there are usually two high tides each day. (But not always!)

Diurnal tides: Areas that have one high tide and one low tide are known as diurnal tides. The Gulf of Mexico is an area that generally has one high tide and one low tide each day.

Mixed tides: Areas that experience both diurnal and semi-diurnal tides are considered areas with mixed tides. The US West Coast has mixed tides.

Range of Tide: The difference in the height of tide during a tidal cycle is the range of tide. For example, if the height of the tide at high water is 8 feet and the height of the tide at low water is 1.5 feet, the range of the tide is, 8 ft. – 1.5 ft.= 6.5 feet.

Stand of the Tide: That short period of time at high water and low water where the water is neither rising nor falling.

Spring Tide: At the full moon and the new moon, the Earth and Moon are in line accentuating the effects of gravity. Spring Tides result in higher high waters and lower low waters resulting in an increased range of tide at this time.

Neap Tide: During the first and last quarter of the moon, the gravitational effect of the moon and sun are at right angles to each other resulting in a reduced gravitational influence. During these times, the height of the tide is lower during high water and higher during low water, resulting in a reduced range of tide.

CALCULATION OF THE HEIGHT OF TIDE AT ANY TIME

Tables

Tide Tables for the United States are published by the National Oceanic and Atmospheric Administration (NOAA). Information on tides along the US coastline can be found at http://tidesandcurrents.noaa.gov/ or in the Tide Tables published annually for each coast.

To calculate the height of tide at any time it may be necessary to use all three of the tables below:

1. The Daily Pages of the appropriate reference station, Table I

2. The corrections for the sub-station as listed in Table II

3. Height of Tide at any time is calculated using Table III

Example   **Find the height of the tide at 1530 in Port Jefferson, New York, on March 2. Using the extracts from the tables shown in Appendix 1.**

Steps   1. Find Port Jefferson- (check the index for station number). Port Jefferson is a subsidiary station (Table II) with Bridgeport, Connecticut, as the daily page reference station (Table I).

2. Find the heights of high and low water at Bridgeport on March 2.

3. Apply corrections found in Table II, Port Jefferson, to "build" the day at Port Jefferson

4. Calculate inputs needed for Table III-
   Range of tide
   Difference in time between high and low water
   Difference in time from nearest high or low water

Question   On March 2, what will be the height of the tide in Port Jefferson, New York, at 1530?

The reference station for Port Jefferson, NY, is the daily page for Bridgeport, Connecticut, with high and low tides on March 2 as shown below taken from Table I:

Bridgeport, CT (Daily Page)	
0105	7.3 HW
0725	-1.3 LW
1332	6.9 HW
1944	-0.9 LW

Time and Height Corrections for Port Jefferson as taken from Table II:

Correction for Times:	Correction for Heights:
High water +0 hr. 6 min.	High - 0.1
Low water +0 hr. 3 min.	Low 0.0

Calculate Times of high and low tide at Port Jefferson, New York
   Add 6 minutes to all Bridgeport times for high water and 3 minutes to low water. This will give the time for each event at Port Jefferson.

Ref. Station Time	Correction	Time at Sub Station (Port Jefferson)
0105	+6 min	0111
0725	+3 min	0728
1332	+6 min	1338
1944	+3 min	1947

Height of Tide at Port Jefferson: Apply correction above

Subtract 0.1 foot from the high water height and 0.0 from the low water to get the heights of high and low tide at Port Jefferson.

```
7.3 HW  -0.1  =   7.2
-1.3 LW   0.0  =  -1.3
6.9 HW  -0.1  =   6.8
-0.9 LW   0.0  =  -0.9
```

Calculated High and Low Tide at Port Jefferson

Time	Tide
0111	7.2 HW
0728	-1.3 LW
1338	6.8 HW
1947	-0.9 LW

Height of Tide at 1530 (03:30 PM) at Port Jefferson:

Range of tide (between high and low)
= 7.7 ft. (6.8 + -0.9)
Duration of rise and fall
= 6 hr – 09 min (1947 – 1338)
Time from nearest high or low
= 1 hr – 52 min (1530 – 1338)

Using Table III, in Appendix 1, find the correction by entering the table with the value nearest the computed intervals above. The correction is the intersection of the row and column in the upper portion of the table carried down the column until the row for the appropriate Range of tide. Enter Table III in Appendix 1 using the value in the table nearest to those above, enter with duration of rise and fall (6:00) move across to (1:48) and then down in the same column to the range of tide (7.5).

Nearest high or Low-	6.9
Correction for Table III-	-1.5
Height of tide at 1530-	5.4 Ft

This number, 5.4 ft, is added to the chart soundings to get the depth of the water at 1530.

Height Of Tide Work Sheet

1. Use the steps below to calculate the times of high and low tide. Find subsidiary station from Tide Tables, Table II. Enter corrections here:

	Time		Height
High Water	Low Water	High Water	Low Water

2. Find times **of high and low tide** at the reference station on the daily pages, Table I, and add or subtract the subsidiary correction from above.

AM Tides-time

Time of 1st high or low: _____

Table II correction: +/- _____

A-Time at sub. Station

Time of 2nd high or low: _____

Table II correction: +/- _____

B-Time at sub. Station

AM Tides-height

Height of 1st high or low: _____

able II correction: +/- _____

Height at sub. station

Height of 2nd high or low: _____

Table II correction: +/- _____

Height at sub. station

PM Tides-time

Time of 3rd high or low: _____

Table II correction: +/- _____

C-Time at sub. station

Time of 4th high or low: _____

Table II correction: +/- _____

D-Time at sub. station

PM Tides-height

Height of 3rd high or low _____

Table II correction: +/- _____

Height at sub. station

Height of 4th high or low _____

Table II correction: +/- _____

Height at sub. station

Daily Summary

A-Time at sub. Station _____

B-Time at sub. Station _____

C-Time at sub. Station _____

D-Time at sub. Station _____

Height at sub. Station _____

Height at sub. Station _____

Height at sub. Station _____

Height at sub. Station _____

BRIDGEPORT, CONN., 1983
Times and Heights of High and Low Waters

	JANUARY							FEBRUARY							MARCH					
	Time	Height			Time	Height			Time	Height			Time	Height			Time	Height		
Day				Day				Day				Day				Day				Day		
	h m	ft	m		h m	ft	m		h m	ft	m		h m	ft	m		h m	ft	m		h m	ft	m
1	0004	6.8	2.1	16	0016	6.2	1.9	1	0131	7.0	2.1	16	0057	6.6	2.0	1	0017	7.3	2.2	16	0606	-0.16	-0.2
Sa	0612	-0.8	-0.2	Su	0621	0.1	0.0	Tu	0747	-1.1	-0.3	W	0710	-0.3	-0.1	Tu	0634	-1.4	-0.4	W	1209	6.8	2.1
	1222	7.7	2.3		1227	6.8	2.1		1355	7.0	2.1		1313	6.6	2.0		1243	7.2	2.2		1821	-0.4	-0.1
	1849	-1.4	-0.4		1848	-0.3	-0.1		2014	-1.1	-0.3		1928	-0.3	-0.1		1857	-1.2	-0.4				
2	0059	6.8	2.1	17	0051	6.3	1.9	2	0224	6.9	2.1	17	0134	6.6	2.0	2	0105	7.3	2.2	17	0027	7.0	2.1
Su	0707	-0.7	-0.2	M	0659	0.2	0.1	W	0842	-0.8	-0.2	Th	0750	-1.3	-0.4	W	0725	-1.3	-0.4	Th	0644	-0.6	-0.2
	1318	7.5	2.3		1302	6.7	2.0		1450	6.6	2.0		1352	6.4	2.0		1332	6.9	2.1		1249	6.6	2.0
	1944	-1.2	-0.4		1923	-0.2	-0.1		2106	-0.7	-0.2		2006	-0.2	-0.1		1944	-0.9	-0.3		1857	-0.3	-0.1
3	0155	6.8	2.1	18	0128	6.3	1.9	3	0319	6.7	2.0	18	0216	6.6	2.0	3	0153	7.0	2.1	18	0105	7.0	2.1
M	0806	-0.6	-0.2	Tu	0736	0.2	0.1	Th	0941	-0.6	-0.2	F	0834	-0.1	0.0	Th	0815	-1.0	-0.3	F	0725	-0.5	-0.2
	1415	7.1	2.2		1341	6.5	2.0		1546	6.1	1.9		1439	6.1	1.9		1421	6.4	2.0		1332	6.4	2.0
	2040	-0.9	-0.3		2000	-0.1	0.0		2200	-0.5	-0.2		2048	0.0	0.0		2034	-0.5	-0.2		1937	-0.1	0.0
4	0251	6.7	2.0	19	0208	6.3	1.9	4	0414	6.5	2.0	19	0303	6.6	2.0	4	0243	6.8	2.1	19	0150	7.0	2.1
Tu	0906	-0.4	-0.1	W	0819	0.3	0.1	F	1039	-0.3	-0.1	Sa	0925	0.0	0.0	F	0908	-0.6	-0.2	Sa	0811	-0.4	-0.1
	1514	6.7	2.0		1422	6.3	1.9		1645	5.7	1.8		1530	5.9	1.8		1512	6.0	1.8		1418	6.2	1.9
	2135	-0.6	-0.2		2040	0.0	0.0		2258	0.0	0.0		2139	0.2	0.1		2125	-0.1	0.0		2023	0.1	0.0
5	0350	6.6	2.0	20	0249	6.3	1.9	5	0513	6.3	1.9	20	0357	6.5	2.0	5	0335	6.5	2.0	20	0237	6.8	2.1
W	1009	-0.3	-0.1	Th	0904	0.3	0.1	Sa	1141	-0.1	0.0	Su	1025	0.1	0.0	Sa	1003	-0.2	-0.1	Su	0904	-0.1	0.0
	1615	6.3	1.9		1509	6.1	1.9		1746	5.5	1.7		1630	5.6	1.7		1608	5.7	1.7		1512	5.9	1.8
	2234	-0.4	-0.1		2122	0.1	0.0		2356	0.2	0.1		2238	0.4	0.1		2220	0.3	0.1		2117	0.4	0.1

					TABLE 2. - TIDAL DIFFERANCES AND OTHER CONSTANTS, 1983							
		POSITION				DIFFERENCES				RANGES		Mean Tide Level
NO.	PLACE	Lat.		Long.		Time		Height				
						High Water	Low Water	High Water	Low Water	Mean	Spring	
		° ' N		° ' W		h. m.	h. m.	ft.	ft.	ft.	ft.	ft.
	New York, East River Time meridian, 75°W					on WILLETS POINT, p.52						
1283	Lawrence Point	40	47	73	55	-0 03	+0 13	-0.7	0.0	6.4	7.6	3.2
1285	Wolcott Avenue	40	47	73	55	-0 03	+0 13	-1.0	0.0	6.1	7.2	3.0
						on NEW YORK, p.56						
1287	Pot Cove Astoria	40	47	73	56	+2 20	+2 29	+0.8	0.0	5.3	6.3	2.6
1289	Hell Gate, Hallets Point	40	47	73	56	+2 00	+2 04	+0.6	0.0	5.1	6.1	2.5
1291	Horns Hook, East 90th Street	40	47	73	57	+1 50	+1 30	+0.3	0.0	4.8	5.8	2.4
1293	Welfare Island, north end	40	46	73	56	+1 45	+1 25	+0.3	0.0	4.8	5.8	2.4
1295	37th Avenue, Long Island City	40	46	73	57	+1 30	+1 10	0.0	0.0	4.5	5.5	2.2
1297	East 41st Street, New York City	40	45	73	58	+1 20	+0 56	-0.2	0.0	4.3	5.2	2.1
1299	Hunters Point, Newtown Creek	40	44	73	57	+1 18	+0 53	-0.4	0.0	4.1	4.9	2.0
1301	English Kills entrance, Newtown Creek	40	43	73	55	+1 30	+1 04	-0.3	0.0	4.2	5.0	2.1
1303	East 27th Street, Bellevue Hospital	40	44	73	58	+1 08	+1 03	-0.3	0.0	4.2	5.0	2.1
1305	East 19th Street, New York City	40	44	73	58	+1 02	+0 58	-0.4	0.0	4.1	4.9	2.0
1307	North 3d Street, Brooklyn	40	43	73	58	+0 55	+0 42	-0.4	0.0	4.1	4.9	2.0
1309	Williamsburg Bridge	40	43	73	58	+0 52	+0 38	-0.4	0.0	4.1	4.9	2.0
1311	Wallabout Bay	40	42	73	59	+0 50	+0 35	-0.4	0.0	4.1	4.9	2.0
1313	Brooklyn Bridge	40	42	73	00	+0 13	+0 07	-0.2	0.0	4.3	5.2	2.1
	Harlem River											
1315	East 110th Street, New York City	40	47	73	56	+1 52	+1 35	+0.6	0.0	5.1	6.1	2.6
1317	Willis Avenue Bridge	40	48	73	56	+1 47	+1 30	+0.5	0.0	5.0	6.0	2.5
1319	Madison Avenue Bridge	40	49	73	56	+1 52	+1 35	+0.4	0.0	4.9	5.9	2.4
1321	Central Bridge	40	50	73	56	+1 52	+1 35	+0.2	0.0	4.7	5.7	2.3
1323	Washington Bridge	40	51	73	56	+1 52	+1 35	-0.1	0.0	4.4	5.2	2.2
1325	University Heights Bridge	40	52	73	55	+1 40	+1 30	-0.5	0.0	4.0	4.8	2.0
1327	Broadway Bridge	40	52	73	55	+1 20	+1 20	-0.7	0.0	3.8	3.8	1.9
1329	Spuyten Duyvil Bridge	40	53	73	56	+1 01	+1 03	-0.9	0.0	3.6	3.6	1.8
	Long Island Sound South Side					on WILLETS POINT, p.52						
1331	WILLETS POINT	40	48	73	47	Daily predictions				7.1	8.3	3.5
1333	Hewlett Point	40	50	73	45	-0 03	-0 03	0.0	0.0	7.1	8.3	3.5
1335	Port Washington, Manhasset Bay	40	50	73	42	-0 01	+0 11	+0.2	0.0	7.3	8.6	3.6
1337	Execution Rocks	40	53	73	44	-0 06	-0 08	+0.2	0.0	7.3	8.6	3.6
1339	Glen Cove, Hempstead Harbor	40	52	73	39	-0 11	-0 06	+0.2	0.0	7.3	8.6	3.6
						on BRIDGEPORT, p.48						
	Oyster Bay											
1341	Oyster Bay Harbor	40	53	73	32	+0 08	+0 11	+0.6	0.0	7.3	8.4	3.6
1343	Bayville Bridge	40	54	73	33	+0 13	+0 18	+0.7	0.0	7.4	8.5	3.7
1345	Cold Spring Harbor	40	52	73	28	+0 08	+0 06	+0.7	0.0	7.4	8.5	3.7
1347	Eatons Neck Point	40	57	73	24	+0 03	+0 06	+0.4	0.0	7.1	8.2	3.6
1349	Lloyd Harbor entrance, Huntington Bay	40	55	73	26	+0 03	+0 01	+0.7	0.0	7.4	8.5	3.7
1351	Northport, Northport Bay	40	54	73	21	+0 03	+0 06	+0.6	0.0	7.3	8.4	3.6
1353	Nisssequogue River entrance	40	54	73	14	-0 03	-0 06	+0.3	0.0	7.0	8.0	3.5
1355	Stony Brook, Smithtown Bay	40	55	73	09	+0 08	+0 08	-0.6	0.0	6.1	7.0	3.0
1357	Stratford Shoal	41	04	73	06	-0 05	-0 09	-0.1	0.0	6.6	7.6	3.3
1359	Port Jefferson Harbor entrance	40	58	73	05	+0 03	-0 01	-0.1	0.0	6.6	7.6	3.3
1361	Port Jefferson	40	57	73	05	+0 06	+0 03	-0.1	0.0	6.6	7.6	3.3
1363	Setauket Harbor	40	57	73	06	+0 04	+0 09	0.0	0.0	6.7	7.7	3.3
1365	Conscience Bay entrance (Narrows)	40	58	73	07	+0 02	+0 02	0.0	0.0	6.7	7.7	3.3
1367	Mount Sinai Harbor	40	58	73	02	+0 05	+0 16	-0.7	0.0	6.0	6.9	3.0
1369	Herod Point	40	58	72	50	-0 07	-0 16	-0.8	0.0	5.9	6.8	2.9
1370	Northville	40	59	72	39	-0 02	-0 05	-1.3	0.0	5.4	6.2	2.7
1371	Mattituck Inlet	41	01	72	34	+0 05	-0 06	-1.5	0.0	5.2	6.0	2.6
1373	Horton Point	41	05	72	27	-0 20	-0 35	*0.60	*0.60	4.0	4.6	2.0
1374	Hashamount Beach	41	06	72	24	+0 04	-0 15	*0.63	*0.63	4.2	4.8	2.1
1375	Truman Beach	41	08	72	19	-0 42	-0 52	*0.51	*0.51	3.4	3.9	1.7

CALCULATING TIDAL CURRENTS

Tidal currents are those currents that are caused by the horizontal movement of the tides. As described below, flood currents are currents that flow towards the land and ebb currents are those that flow away from the land. These are generally called reversing currents and move opposite each other. Reversing are the most common tidal currents, the kind of current that flows up the tidal creek during a rising tide and down the tidal creek during a falling tide.

Depending on the geographic location, tidal currents can be minimal or strong and dangerous. When making a landfall in an area that has a significant range of tide, the mariner must assume a strong tidal current and plan accordingly. In some cases, arrivals and departures are planned for the time of minimal current, slack water, to make ship handling and maneuvering less hazardous. For low power vessels, such as many sailboats, moving against the tidal current in some areas is simply not an option.

▶ **Important Tidal Current Definitions**

Reversing Current: Most tidal currents are considered Reversing Currents. The current flows towards the land from seaward during Flood current, and then reverses the direction of flow by 180° at the Ebb. Reversing currents have only two directions of flow, in and out.

Rotary Currents: Rotary currents, unlike those above, change direction through 360° over the course of a tidal cycle. Nautical charts note areas where rotary currents are present with a current rose. Rotary currents can also be calculated at any time using the tables in the back of the Tide Tables published by NOAA.

Flood Current: The flood current is that cycle of the current that flows in from the sea towards land.

Ebb Current: The ebb current is that cycle of the current that flows towards the ocean away from the land.

Slack Water: Slack water is that relatively short period of time before the current changes direction when there is little or no current. This is the time around which arrivals and departures, or transits, are planned in areas with strong tidal currents.

Finding the strength of the current at any time: Like the tide tables, current tables are divided into three parts

1. Daily Tables of selected reference stations **(Table I)**. Note that times are always shown in standard Zone Time and must be adjusted for Daylight Savings Time, DST, **(one time zone ahead)**. **Note:** The tide tables used on U.S. Coast Guard texts are shown in standard zone time. Actual tide tables published by NOAA are usually adjusted to local time.

2. Subsidiary Stations **(Table II)**

3. Strength of Current at Any Time **(Table III)**
    To calculate the current at any time, Table III must be referenced after calculating the times of maximum current and slack at the subsidiary station.

Caution!

Table III is divided into two separate tables, A and B. Make sure you are using the correct table for your location. **See Appendix 2.**

For example

What is the velocity of the tidal current at the east end of Pollock Rip Channel at 1700 DST (ZD +4) on 23 July?

1. Find Subsidiary station, Table II, reference station and corrections
    1341 Pollack Rip, east end. The reference station is **Pollack Rip Channel**

BF Min Fld	Fld	BF Min Ebb	Ebb	Spd Ratios Fld	Ebb
-0 14	-0 39	-0 23	-0 38	1 0	1 1

2. Find the times at Pollack Rip Channel that are appropriate to the question and adjust for East End location **AND**, in this case, adjust for daylight savings. time (ZD +4)

Slack	Max Current	Knots
0156	0534	2.2F
0835	1131	1.6E
1428	1751	1.9F
2039	2338	1.7E

Before and after times:	1428	1751	1.9F
Adjust for DST: + 1hr.	+1	+1	
	1528	1851	
Corrections, Table II:	- 14	- 39	x 1.0
Pollack Rip East End	1514	1812	1.9 Kts.

3. Table III data:

Interval between slack and max current:
1812 – 1514 = 2 hr 58 min

Interval between slack and desired time:
1700 – 1514 = 1 hr 46 min

Using Table III in Appendix 2, find the correction by entering the table with the value nearest the computed interval (3-00) and (1-40). The correction is the intersection of the row and column.

In this case there is no correction, the table indicates 0. So the current at 1700 is: **1.9 kts. flooding.**

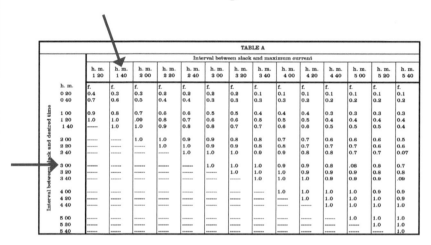

	Interval between slack and maximum current													
h. m.	h. m. 1 20	h. m. 1 40	h. m. 2 00	h. m. 2 20	h. m. 2 40	h. m. 3 00	h. m. 3 20	h. m. 3 40	h. m. 4 00	h. m. 4 20	h. m. 4 40	h. m. 5 00	h. m. 5 20	h. m. 5 40
	f.	f.	f.	f.	f.	f.	f.	f.	f.	f.	f.	f.	f.	f.
0 20	0.4	0.3	0.3	0.2	0.2	0.2	0.2	0.1	0.1	0.1	0.1	0.1	0.1	0.1
0 40	0.7	0.6	0.5	0.4	0.4	0.3	0.3	0.3	0.3	0.2	0.2	0.2	0.2	0.2
1 00	0.9	0.8	0.7	0.6	0.6	0.5	0.5	0.4	0.4	0.4	0.3	0.3	0.3	0.3
1 20	1.0	1.0	.09	0.8	0.7	0.6	0.6	0.5	0.5	0.5	0.4	0.4	0.4	0.4
1 40	------	1.0	1.0	0.9	0.8	0.8	0.7	0.7	0.6	0.6	0.5	0.5	0.5	0.4
2 00	------	------	1.0	1.0	0.9	0.9	0.8	0.8	0.7	0.7	0.6	0.6	0.6	0.5
2 20	------	------	------	1.0	1.0	0.9	0.9	0.8	0.8	0.7	0.7	0.7	0.6	0.6
2 40	------	------	------	------	1.0	1.0	1.0	0.9	0.9	0.8	0.8	0.7	0.7	0.07
3 00	------	------	------	------	------	1.0	1.0	1.0	0.9	0.9	0.8	.08	0.8	0.7
3 20	------	------	------	------	------	------	1.0	1.0	1.0	0.9	0.9	0.9	0.8	0.8
3 40	------	------	------	------	------	------	------	1.0	1.0	1.0	0.9	0.9	0.9	.09
4 00	------	------	------	------	------	------	------	------	1.0	1.0	1.0	1.0	0.9	0.9
4 20	------	------	------	------	------	------	------	------	------	1.0	1.0	1.0	1.0	0.9
4 40	------	------	------	------	------	------	------	------	------	------	1.0	1.0	1.0	1.0
5 00	------	------	------	------	------	------	------	------	------	------	------	1.0	1.0	1.0
5 20	------	------	------	------	------	------	------	------	------	------	------	------	1.0	1.0
5 40	------	------	------	------	------	------	------	------	------	------	------	------	------	1.0

TABLE A

Interval between slack and desired time

CHAPTER FOUR
THE SAILINGS

Plotting a course over the horizon or across an ocean requires the use of a set of equations known as "the sailings." When traveling great distances, there is the need to calculate course and distance over the earth, from the latitude and longitude of departure to the latitude and longitude of arrival. Short distances may be calculated directly on a chart, but long distances can be solved accurately using the equations below.

A Little Background

Almost all charts used in day-to-day navigation are Mercator projections. In an effort to keep angular relationships between landmasses accurate and project a round earth on a flat surface, the Mercator projection uses a cylindrical method of projection. A Mercator chart expands lines of latitude as they go north and south from where the cylinder is tangent to the earth. In this way, the higher the latitude, the more expanded it appears on the chart. Over small areas this isn't much of a problem, but over a large area, like a Mercator projection of the northern hemisphere, the distortion can be huge.

As the projection goes further north, the lines of latitude are expanded until they literally go off the chart.

MERCATOR SAILING

The Mercator sailing is based on the fact that a rhumb line, which shows as a straight line on a Mercator chart projection, is actually a loxodromic curve. The loxodromic curve, if plotted on the face of the earth, would spiral in a curve towards the poles. To counter this, and keep us sailing a straight course, Mercator sailing uses the principal of expanding latitude relationships, meridional parts, to keep course lines constant between distant points on the earth.

All mercator sailing problems are based on the trigonometric relationships shown below. These formulas can be used to solve any mercator sailing problem.

Important!

The answer obtained from the formulas is the **Course Angle**, not the actual course. It is necessary to change the course angle obtained from the formula to the actual course to steer.

Course angle can be found by looking at direction of travel. North or South as a prefix, and then East or West as a suffix. For example, if the destination is north and east of the point of departure then the course angle would be North and East. If the point of arrival is south and west of the point of departure then the course angle would be labeled South and West.

Course is calculated differently by quadrant:

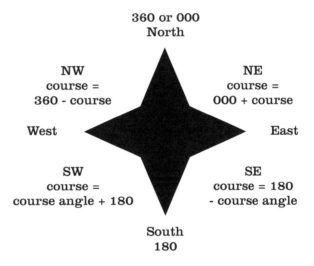

360 or 000
North

NW
course =
360 - course

NE
course =
000 + course

West

East

SW
course =
course angle + 180

SE
course = 180
- course angle

South
180

Course Angle Example

A true course of 121° would have a Course Angle of S 59° E

180° - 59°= 121°

A true course of 350° would have a Course Angle of N 10° W

360° - 10° = 350°

To find course and distance to a destination when given departure and arrival latitude and longitude, use the following formula:

Tan C = DLO/DM
D= Dlat/Cos C

To find new Latitude and Longitude when given departure Lat/long and Course and Distance, use the following formula:

Dlat = Cos C x D

Dlo =DM x Tan C

Where

C = Course Angle

DM = Difference in Meridional Parts

DLO = Difference in Longitude

P = Departure

Dlat = Difference in Latitude

Dist = Distance

All formulas relate to this triangle showing a south & east relationship.

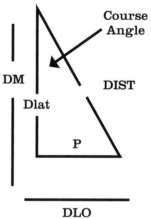

Cosine of the course angle = adjacent/hypotenuse

Cosine Course Angle = Dlat/DIST

Tangent of the course angle = opposite/adjacent

Tangent of the Course Angle = DLO/DM

Mercator Sailing Examples: Problem 1

Depart Lat 40° - 42 N, Long 74°- 01 W and steam 3,365.6 miles on course 118° T. What is the Longitude of arrival?

Course Angle (Cn)= 180° – 118° = 62°, S 62 E
Distance = 3,365.6

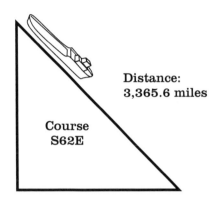

Distance:
3,365.6 miles

Course
S62E

First, find Dlat

1. Formula to use:

   Cos C= Dlat/ Dist or Dlat= Cos C x Dist

Action 2

Dlat = Cosine 62 x 3,365.6

   Dlat = .46947 x 3,365.6= 1,580

Action 3

Answer is in minutes so divide by 60 to get degrees

   Dlat= 1,580/60= 26.335 ° or 26°

Action 4

Change decimal to minutes

   Dlat= 60 minutes x .335= 20.1   Dlat= 26°- 20.1'

Action 5

Action, Find new latitude

   Lat 1- 40° - 42.0 N
   -Dlat   26° - 20.1
   Lat 2- 14° - 21.9 N

Second, calculate Dlong

1. Formula to use:

$$\text{Tan C} = \text{Dlo/DM}$$

Action 2

Solve for Dlo

$$\text{Dlo} = \text{Tan C x DM}$$

Find difference of meridional parts (From Meridional parts Table in Bowditch)

Lat 1-	40° - 42.0----	M1- 2,662.6
Lat 2-	14° - 21.9----	M2- 865.3
Diff.	Mer. Parts	1,797.3

Action 3

Multiply Tan C x Difference Meridional Parts

$$\text{Dlo} = 1.88073 \times 1797.3 = 3380.23$$

Action 4

Answer in minutes so divide by 60 to get degrees

$$3380.23 / 60 = 56.34° \text{ or } 56°\text{- } 20.4'$$

Action 5

find new Long

Long1-	74°- 01 W	
-Dlo	56 - 20	easterly heading, subtract
New	17°- 41 W	

Arrival

Latitude: 14° – 21.9, Longitude: 17° – 41

▶ ## Problem 2

A vessel at Lat 37° - 24.0 N and long 178° - 15.0 W heads for a destination at Lat 34° - 18.0 N and Long 178° - 25.0 E. What is the true course and distance by mercator sailing?

Action 1

First calculate:
    Difference of Latitude
    Difference of Meridional Parts
    Difference of Longitude (going across 180 ° West to East, add longitudes and then subtract from 360)

Function	Latitude	Meridional	Longitude
First	37° - 24.0 N	2408.6	178° - 15.0 W
Second	-34° - 18.0 N	-2180.1	+178° - 25.0 E
Difference	3° - 06	228.5	356° - 40.0
			359° - 60.0
			-356° - 40.0
		Dlo	3° - 20.0

Action 2   Change degrees and minutes to minutes

Dlat= (60 x 3 °) + 6 = 186   Dlo= (60 x 3 °) + 20= 200

Action 3   Calculate course

Tan C= Dlo/DM   Tan C = 200/228.5= 0.87527
C (course angle) = 41.2
S 41.2 W
Course = 180 + 41.2= 221.2° True

Action 4   calculate distance

Cos C = Dlat/ D (solve for distance, D)
D = Dlat/Cos C (Cosine 41.2)
D = 186/.7524   Distance = 247.2 miles

MID-LATITUDE SAILING

Mid-latitude sailing formulas split the difference between the expansion of latitude lines on a Mercator chart and use the middle latitude between the departure and arrival latitude. If meridional parts tables aren't available the mid-latitude method is a good substitute. Everything can be done with these three equations:

1- P= Dlo x Cos Lm   2- TanC=P/DL   3- D= DL/Cos C

Where   Lm = the middle latitude between departure and arrival. If departure is 20° and arrival is 10° than the Lm is 15°.

DL = the Difference of Latitude
    between departure and arrival
Dlo = difference of longitude
P = departure in nautical miles
C = course angle

Examples   1. You depart LAT 28°55.0'N, LONG 89°10.0'W, en route to LAT 24°25.0'N, LONG 83°00.0'W. Determine the true course and distance by mid-latitude sailing?

Action 1   Calculate the difference of latitude, the mid-latitude and the difference of longitude.

Lat 1- 28°-55.0'N   Long 1- 89°- 10.0'W
Lat 2- 24°-25.0'N   Long 2- 83°- 00.0'W
DL   4°-30   Dlo   6°- 10.0

In minutes= Lat (4° x 60)+ 30=270'
Long (6° x 60) + 10= 370'

Mean Lat.=
One half of the Dl of 4° 30 = 2° - 15,
                 28°- 55 N
              + 2°- 15
Mean lat.   26°- 40 or 26.6666°

Action 2   Using the three formulas above

P= Dlo x Cos Lm   P= 370 x Cos 26.6666= 330.6 (.893637)

Solve for course angle C

Tan C=P/DL   Tan C= 330.6/270= 1.22461   C= 50.8

Course angle = S 50.8 E or 129° T Course to steer

D= DL/Cos C   D= 270/Cos (.632029) C   D= 427 miles

Example   A vessel steams 580 miles on course 083°T from LAT 13°12'N, LONG 71°12'W. What are the latitude and longitude of the point of arrival by mid-latitude sailing?

Action 1   calculate destination latitude

D= DL/Cos C or DL= D x Cos C   DL = 580 x Cos
83 ° (.12187) = 70.68' or 1° - 11'
  Lat 1- 13° - 12'N
+ DL   1° - 11
New Lat 14° - 23   LM=   1° - 11 x ½ = 35.5'
                         LM= 13° - 47.5 or 13.792°

Action 2   calculate destination longitude

TanC=P/DL or P= Tan C x DL
P= Tan 83° x 70.86= 575.6
   (8.1443)
DLO= P/ Cos LM DLO= 575.6/.9712= 592.7'
(change to degrees and minutes)
592.7/ 60= 9.87° or 9° - 53

Long1=   71° - 12 W
    - DLO 9° - 53   subtract for easterly course
New Long. 61° - 19 W

PARALLEL SAILING

Before the development of the chronometer, finding longitude was difficult when it could be done at all. In those days, mariners would go north or south to the latitude of their destination and then sail due east or west, along a parallel of latitude, until they reached their destination. Mariners could find their latitude with a noon sight.

Although for different reasons, parallel sailing is still an option in some voyage plans and is calculated as shown below.

Parallel sailing is only used when course is due east (090°) or west (270°).

P= DLO x Cos lat

Where P is departure, or distance in nautical miles, between the longitude of departure and the longitude of arrival. Because lines of longitude are not parallel, but intersect at the poles, the distance between any given two lines of longitude is different as Latitude changes.

DLO (Difference of Longitude) is entered in minutes. For example a DLO of 30°- 30' would equal 1,830 minutes (30° x 60 = 1,800', 1,800 + 30= 1,830').

Example   **A vessel is leaving longitude 009°- 15' W and heading for 025°- 10' W. The vessel will steam along Latitude 35°- 30' N. What is the distance in nautical miles?**

1 DLO=   025°- 10'
               - 009°- 15'
                 015°- 55' or 955 minutes

2 P=   Cos   35.5° x 955' = 777.5 nautical miles.

GREAT CIRCLE SAILING

The shortest distance between any two points on the earth is a **great circle**. A great circle is defined as a circle around the earth that runs through the center and cuts the earth into equal half's. The equator is an example of a great circle as are all lines of longitude. Lines of latitude, with the exception of the equator, are called **small circles**.

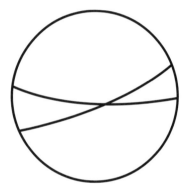

Since it is impossible to actually steer a curve, Great Circle sailing involves first outlining the circle by finding waypoints and then steering a straight line, a rhumb line course, between the waypoints.

The two ways of calculating a great circle route without the use of an electronic chart program are:

1. Using a gnomonic, or great circle, chart

2. Calculating the points along the curve

▶ **Gnomonic Charts**

On a gnomonic chart projection a straight line is a great circle. If a line is drawn between the point of departure and the point of arrival and then the points along that line, say every five or ten degrees of longitude, are transferred to a Mercator projection of the same area, the result would be to show the arc of the great circle on the Mercator projection. Once these waypoints are plotted, then a rhumb line course is steered between each waypoint.

In this way the curve of the great circle is approximated by steering a series of straight lines between waypoints.

Great Circle by Computation

Calculating the great circle course by formula is a good deal of work and requires that the navigator be accurate and careful with their calculations. Shown below are all the formulas, with examples. In the appendix is a fully worked out example.

Great Circle Calculation Rules

1. Distance calculation: If Lat of departure is different from Lat of arrival (i.e., crossing the equator) then Sin L2 is treated as a negative quantity.

2. Initial Course Calculation: If Lat of departure is different from Lat of arrival (i.e., crossing the equator) then Tan L2 is treated as a negative number.

3. Initial Course Calculation: If Tan C is a negative number, then add 180 to result to obtain course angle.

4. Course Angle: Course angle, N or S, is determined by the label of the departure latitude. E or W is determined by the direction of travel.

▶ ### Great Circle Formulas

Initial Course and Distance-

$$\text{Cos D} = (\text{Sin L1} \times \text{Sin L2*}) + (\text{Cos L1} \times \text{Cos L2} \times \text{Cos Dlo})$$

$$\text{Tan C} = \frac{\text{Sin Dlo}}{(\text{Cos L1} \times \text{Tan L2*}) \quad - \quad (\text{Sin L1} \times \text{Cos Dlo})}$$

* **negative when crossing the equator**

Finding the Latitude and Longitude of the Vertex

Lat of the vertex- $\text{Cos Lv} = \text{Cos L1} \times \text{Sin C}$

Long of the vertex- $\text{Sin Dlov} = \text{Cos C} / \text{Sin LV}$

Note

C is the Course angle, not the true course

Dlov is the difference of longitude between the point of departure and the vertex. This is added or subtracted depending on direction of travel

Distance from the point of Departure to the Vertex-

$$\text{Sin Dv} = \text{Cos L1} \times \text{Sin Dlov}$$

Finding Points along the Great Circle Track (X)

The Latitude of a point X along the great circle track:

Tan Lx= Cos Dlovx x Tan Lv
or
Sin Lx= Sin Lv x Cos Dvx

Note

Dlovx is the difference of longitude between the vertex and point X. If given in miles convert to degrees (1° equals 60 miles. Example: X is 600 miles from the vertex, 600/60 = 10°).

The Longitude of point X along the Great Circle track:

$$\text{Sin Dlovx} = \frac{\text{Sin Dvx}}{\text{Cos Lx}}$$

Great Circle Example

Distance: Determine the great circle distance and initial course from LAT 24°52.0'N, LONG 78°27.0'W to LAT 47°19.0'N, LONG 06°42.0'W.

Cos D= (Sin L1 x Sin L2*) + (Cos L1 x Cos L2 x Cos Dlo)
Cos D = (Sin 24°52.0 x Sin 47°19.0)
    + (Cos 24°52.0x Cos 47°19.0 x Cos 71- 45)
Cos D= .501745
D= 59.88 ° x 60 = 3593 miles

Note

Since one minute equals one nautical mile on a great circle, the total number of minutes equals the number of miles.

Initial Course

$$\text{Tan C} = \frac{\text{Sin Dlo}}{(\text{Cos L1 x Tan L2*}) - (\text{Sin L1 x Cos Dlo})}$$

$$\text{Tan C} = \frac{\text{Sin 71° -45}}{(\text{Cos 24°-52 x Tan 47°-19}) - (\text{Sin 24°-52.0 x Cos 71° - 45})}$$

Tan C=   1.11455
C=   48.1 °
Course Angle=   N 48.1 E= 048.1° T

Latitude
and Longitude
of the Vertex

1   Lat of the vertex - Cos Lv = Cos L1 x Sin C
    CosLv = Cos 24 °-52 X Sin 48.1 ° = .675304
    Lat of Vertex = 47.5 ° N

2   Dif Long of the vertex- Sin Dlov
    = Cos C/Sin LV = .905817

    Difference of Long from departure to the vertex
    = 64.93° or 64° - 56'

    Longitude of the vertex= 13° - 31' W

      78 °-27 W
     -64 °-56 W
      13 °-31 W

Finding Points (Waypoints) along the Great Circle Track

A great circle track is really a series of rhumb lines (straight courses) sailed between waypoints along the Great Circle track. Use the formulas below to find waypoints along the track.

Example

Assume we want to set waypoints every 10 degrees from our vertex (it could be any degrees or even miles).

The Latitude of a point X along the Great Circle track can be found below where Dlovx is the difference of longitude between the vertex and any point we choose. In this case every 10 degrees. Lv is the Latitude of the vertex.

Tan Lx=	Cos Dlovx	x Tan Lv	=Lat.of waypoint
(10° away)	Cos 10°	Tan 47.5	47.06°
		(1.074727)	
(20° away)	Cos 20°	Tan 47.5	45.72°
		(1.025494)	
(30° away)	Cos 30°	Tan 47.5	43.38°
		(.9451005)	

CHAPTER FIVE

COMMON CALCULATIONS IN CELESTIAL NAVIGATION

"Navigation is easy. If it wasn't, they wouldn't
be able to teach it to sailors."

—James Lawrence

The calculations and examples shown below are still required knowledge for any Mate or Master seeking an Ocean's Endorsement on their license and are practiced daily on most ocean going vessels as a back-up to electronic methods of navigation. Being able to fix the vessel's position with a sextant and timepiece is still a matter of pride, and maybe necessity, for most professional mariners.

FINDING LATITUDE AT MERIDIAN TRANSIT CALCULATIONS OF LOCAL APPARENT NOON (LAN)

▶ What is Local Apparent Noon (LAN)?

LAN is when the sun, or any celestial body, reaches the mid-point between rising and setting. This is also called Meridian Transit. At this time, it is directly north or south of the ship's position because it is passing over the same longitude (meridian). Because it is directly North or South the Line of Position (LOP) from this sight crosses the meridian at a right angle. The LOP is the vessel's Latitude. Latitude can be calculated using a simple formula shown below and full sight reduction is unnecessary.

▶ Things You Need To Know to Calculate Latitude and LAN and Time of LAN

1. **You must be able to convert Arc to Time to calculate the time of Local Apparent Noon at your particular location.** Celestial navigation makes a number of assumptions that don't exactly agree with the physical reality of the universe. For example, for navigational purposes we assume that the earth revolves at a constant rate and in 24 hours it covers exactly 360° every day. **One day is one full rotation.** Accordingly, the following relationships allow us to convert time to degrees of arc and vice-versa.

> If **24 hours = 360°**,
> then
> One hour (time) = **15° of Arc**
> Four minutes (time) = **1° of Arc**
> One Minute (time) = **15 minutes of Arc**

Arc to Time can be calculated mathematically or by using the Conversion of Arc to Time Table in the back of the Nautical Almanac.

Example   Convert 3°- 15 minutes of Arc to Time

> **3°-15 minutes of arc = 195 minutes of arc**
> **195 minutes/ 15' per Minute of Time = 13 Minutes of Time**

Or Use Table in Nautical Almanac

2. Time of Meridian Passage of the sun is shown on the daily pages of the Nautical Almanac. You can find this at the bottom right hand of each page where time is given for the Sun and the Moon. This time represents the time of Local Apparent Noon (LAN) **at the Central Meridian** in each time zone (i.e., 15°, 30°, 45°, etc. East or West Longitude). Unless you happen to be at that longitude, you will have to correct time for your actual longitude East or West of the central meridian using the Arc-to-Time calculation above.

If you are **East** of the Central Meridian, then you must subtract your calculated time difference from that shown in the Nautical Almanac.

If you are **West** of the Central Meridian, then you must add your calculated time to that found in the Nautical Almanac.

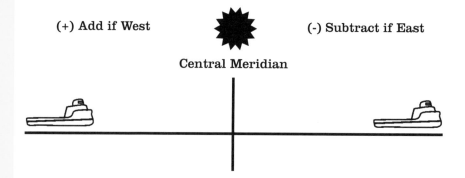

(+) Add if West   **(-) Subtract if East**

Central Meridian

The sun appears to move east to west across the sky, so, if we are east of the central meridian the sun will pass our longitude before it reaches the central meridian and we must subtract that time from the time of meridian passage in the Nautical Almanac. Conversely, we must add time if we are west of the central meridian.

Example:
What is the Time of
LAN at our location?

The Nautical Almanac on Feb. 18 lists Meridian Passage at 1214. Our DR position is Lat 43° – 12 N, Longitude 155° - 25 West.

Calculate Local Time of LAN at our position:

1 ZD = +10, Central Meridian = 150° (155°-25'/15°)

2 The difference between our DR Long.
       and the Central Meridian = 5°- 25' West

3 Arc to Time: 5°- 25' = 21 minutes- 40 seconds <u>of time</u>

4 Time of LAN is
       1214
       <u>+ 21-40</u>
       1235-40

1235-40 is the time of LAN at our location

CALCULATION OF LOCAL APPARENT NOON (LAN) OF THE SUN

Traditionally the Noon sight is the most important fix of the day. The vessel's Noon Report calculates distance run from noon to noon, fuel consumption, slip, and other important information. Although it is called the Noon sight, this is a bit of a misnomer as meridian transit rarely occurs at exactly 1200, instead it can be as much as 20 minutes before or after 1200. The line of position gotten as a result of a LAN sight is usually run up or back to 1200 to get a 1200 running fix.

The noon sight is important because when taken at LAN, it gives Latitude as a line of position.

To calculate your latitude at LAN, first calculate the <u>time of LAN at your location</u>. Then, follow the formula:

    89°- 60 (90°)
    <u>-HO (Height Observed*)</u>
    ZD (Zenith Distance)
    <u>Dec.+/- Declination: Corrected from the daily pages at GMT</u>
    Lat. Line of position is your Latitude
    *Corrected Sextant Altitude (see section on sight reduction)

Example:
Using
the data
above

1. First find GMT and declination

Time of LAN is:	12-35-40 LT	
ZD +	10	
GMT	22 -35-40	February 18.

Declination @ 2200	S11-24.7	From Nautical Almanac
d corr. (0.9)(-)	.5	
Dec. @ 22-35-40	S11-24.2	

2. Sextant Observed Altitude (HO)

This is the sextant altitude (HO) **AFTER** all corrections have been made.

HO =	35°- 25	
	89°- 60	
HO(-)	35°- 25	Height Observed: <u>Corrected Sextant Altitude</u>
ZD	54°- 35	Zenith Distance
Dec.+/-	11°- 24.2	Declination: <u>Corrected from the daily pages</u>
Lat.	43° -10.8	Line of position is the <u>Latitude at the time of the sight</u>

CALCULATION OF
SUNRISE AND SUNSET

Calculation of sunrise and sunset is done very much like the calculation for LAN but there needs to be an additional interpellation for your correct Latitude at the time of the event.

For example, a typical page in the Nautical Almanac gives the times of nautical twilight, civil twilight, and sunrise as shown in the table below.

Lat	Nautical	Civil	Sunrise
N40	0431	0503	0531
35	0439	0510	0535
30	0446	0515	0539
20	0457	0523	0545
N 10	0505	0529	0551

All times are zone times at the central meridian

▶ Steps to Calculate time of sunrise

1. Determine your latitude to the nearest degree at about the time of sunrise. For example, if you estimate your latitude is 38 north then the time of sunrise at the central meridian would be:

Interpolation- (2°/5°) x 4 minutes
= 1.6 minutes (round to 2 minutes)

Difference

$$5° \left\{ \begin{array}{l} \text{Table } \left[\begin{array}{l} 40° \text{ N} \qquad 0531 \\ 2° \\ \text{Pos. } 38° \text{ N} \end{array} \right. \\ \text{Table} \qquad 35° \text{ N} \qquad 0535 \end{array} \right\} 4 \text{ minutes}$$

Estimated Time for Latitude 38N =–
0531 + 2= 0533

2. Change difference of arc to time based on the distance in arc from our longitude position to the central meridian.

For example, if we were at 25° E longitude our central meridian would be 30° E.

We are 5° of arc west of the central meridian, which equates to 20 minutes of time.

5° of arc = 20 minutes of time

Our position is west of the central meridian so time is added.

0533 + 20 minutes= 0553 sunrise at that location

25° E, Our Position   30° E (Central Meridian)

5° arc

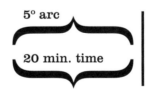

20 min. time

Add time if west   Subtract time if east

CHAPTER SIX

WORKING A CELESTIAL SIGHT: SIGHT REDUCTION

"The true peace of God begins at the point
1,000 miles from the nearest land."

—Joseph Conrad

A FIVE-STEP PROCESS

Here in these few pages is everything you need to know to take a sextant sight of the sun and stars, then "reduce" your sight so a **Line of Position (LOP)** can be plotted. This method uses H.O. 229. Although there are other reduction tables H.O. 229 is what the US Coast Guard uses for their license exams so it is used here.

> ## Think of this as a process with five major steps

1. The first step is to take the sight (Hs), record the exact time the sight is taken, a DR position at the time of the sight and correct the sextant altitude (Ho).

2. The second step is to calculate the Local Hour Angle (LHA) and Declination (Dec.) using information from the Nautical Almanac.

3. Third is to find the calculated height (Hc) and Azimuth (z) from the H.O. 229 for the latitude, LHA, and declination.

4. Fourth, compare the corrected sextant sight, Ho, to the calculated, Hc, to determine the Intercept.

5. Fifth, plot the Line of Position (LOP).

As with any fix based on LOP's two are needed to get a fix. This can be done by either waiting a couple of hours and then taking another sun line and running the first up to the time of the second, a running fix, or taking two celestial bodies at the same time.

> ## Definitions

Knowing the definitions below is critical to understanding the process. Take a minute and read through each of the terms and definitions. The definitions have been grouped into the steps described above.

> ## Step One: The sextant sight—Finding Observed Altitude (Ho)

Sextant Altitude (Hs): This is the actual measurement taken from the sextant. Sextant altitude is the angle of the sun, or other body, above the horizon before any corrections are made.

Index Error (IE): On most sextants there is an inherent error in the instrument. Before each sight is taken, the observer should look through the eye piece and adjust the sextant so that the horizon shows as a straight, unbroken line across both mirrors. When the horizon shows as a straight line, look at the micrometer. The reading will most likely not be exactly at zero but will be a little forward of zero (on the arc) or behind zero (off the arc). It is necessary to correct for this by: subtracting the error if it is on the arch, or, adding the error if it is off the arch.

Height of Eye (Dip): It is necessary to adjust the sight taken with the sextant for the observer's height above the sea surface. This correction is taken from the first page of the Nautical Almanac. This also means the observer has to know what their height of eye is when taking the sight.

Altitude Correction (Ha): After correcting for dip and IE, it is necessary to use the table found in the Nautical Almanac to make the Apparent Altitude correction. The table, usually found on the first page of the Nautical Almanac, is entered for the proper time of year and whether or not the sight was a lower limb or upper limb. Pay attention to the sign of the correction to see whether it is added or subtracted.

Height, Observed (Ho): After all the above corrections are made, the result is Ho. This is the observed altitude that is later compared with the computed altitude to get the line of position.

▶ **Sextant Correction**

After the sight is taken (HS), correct the sight for Index Error and Height of Eye (Dip) to get Apparent Height (Ha). Find Ha correction in the Nautical Almanac to get HO, Height Observed.

Sextant Angle	Hs
Index Error	IE (+/-)
Height of Eye	Dip (-) _____
Apparent Alt.	Ha
Ha Corr.(+/-)	_____
Height Observed	Ho

▶ **Step Two: Finding the Local Hour Angle and Declination from the Nautical Almanac**

Time: The accuracy of your celestial sight is completely dependent on the accuracy of the time used. The time a sight is taken must be observed to the second and any watch error accounted for. If using a chronometer, make sure the chronometer error has been applied. The best bet is to set your watch to the time shown on the GPS, which comes from the atomic clocks imbedded in the satellites. In any case, the wrong time will give the wrong position.

Local Time: The time being kept at the observer's location on the earth.

Zone Description (ZD): The number of hours, added or subtracted, from local time that will give the time at Greenwich (GMT). The earth is divided into 24 separate time zones whose central meridians are multiples of 15 degrees. Each time zone spans 7 ½ degrees on either side of the central meridian. For example, at 30 degrees East or West Longitude, the +/- 2 time zone, the limits of the +/- 2 zone would be from 22 ½° to 37 ½°. Zone Description can be found by dividing longitude by 15 and rounding down if less than 0.5 or up if 0.5 or greater.

If the observer is in west longitude, then the correction to GMT is added to local time and if the observer is in east longitude than the correction is subtracted from local time.

Greenwich Mean Time (GMT): By convention, the time at Greenwich, England, is used in the Nautical Almanac to compute the position of the sun and other celestial bodies. It is necessary to convert the exact local time of the sight to GMT. GMT is also called Universal Time (UT).

When looking up GHAs in the Nautical Almanac always use GMT!

Greenwich Hour Angle (GHA): The GHA is that angle measured in degrees westerly from the Greenwich Meridian to the celestial body being observed. The GHA value must be taken out of the Daily Pages of the Nautical Almanac for the hour, minute, and second that the sight was taken. The hourly amount is taken from the daily page and the additions for minutes and seconds are found in the "**Increments and Corrections**" section towards the end of the Almanac.

Local Hour Angle (LHA): The angle measured westerly in degrees from the observers position to the celestial body. For sight reduction purposes this must be made into a whole number using the DR longitude.

> **LHA = GHA + East Longitude,**
> **or LHA = GHA - West Longitude**

Finding Assumed Longitude and Local Hour Angle

Assumed Longitude: Based on the DR position of the vessel, assumed Longitude is that longitude which gives a whole number LHA when added or subtracted from the GHA. The assumed longitude MUST be within 30 minutes, plus or minus, of the DR longitude.

Example

DR Longitude 45°- 25.5 W the assumed longitude must be between 44°- 55.5 W and 45°-55.5 W (+/- 30 minutes)

If GHA was	135°- 57.7
Then Assumed Long. is minus	44°- 57.7
LHA equals	91°- 00.0

Example   DR Longitude 45°- 25.5 E the assumed longitude must be between 44°- 55.5 E and 45°-55.5 E (+/- 30 minutes)

If GHA was	135° - 57.7
Then Assumed Long. is plus	45° - 02.3
LHA equals	181° - 00.0

Declination: Declination is the angle, north or south of the celestial equator, of the celestial body and can be thought of as the celestial horizon equivalent of Latitude. Declination is found in the daily pages of the Nautical Almanac next to the hourly GHA. Remember to apply the "d" correction for minutes found at the bottom of the Declination column.

▶ Step Three: the Nautical Almanac to Find LHA and Declination

Using the Almanac, determine the LHA of the body and the Declination at the GMT and date of the sight. GHA is found in the daily pages for Hr. and in the "Increments and Corrections" section for minutes and seconds. Declination is found next to GHA in the daily pages, d corr. is found at the bottom of the daily page and then the appropriate correction found in the Increments and Corrections section.

GHA (hr)		Dec.(hr)	
GHA (+ m/s)	_____	d Corr.	_____
Sun GHA		Dec	
+/-A Long	_____		
LHA			

▶ Step Four: Finding the Computed Altitude (Hc) and the Azimuth (Zn) in the HO 229

The three inputs needed to look up the correct Hc and Z in the HO 229 are: LHA, Declination, and Latitude. LHA and Declination come from Step Three, latitude is the Assumed Latitude defined below.

Assumed Latitude: That Latitude which is the nearest whole Latitude to your DR position. This is used in both the Assumed Position and as one of the entries in HO 229.

Example

DR Lat 23°-27 N, Assumed latitude equals 23° N
DR Lat 15°-45 S, Assumed latitude equals 16° S

Height, Calculated (Hc): Hc is the calculated height of the body as taken from the tables in HO 229.

Azimuth (Zn): The horizontal measurement from north or south, depending on the elevated pole, through 360°, which translates into the compass bearing of the celestial body.

Azimuth Angle (Z): The horizontal measurement from north or south depending on the elevated pole, through 180 ° east or west. This, along with Hc, is taken from the tables in HO 229 and must be converted to an azimuth so a line of position can be plotted.

Intercept: The difference in miles between Ho and Hc. This is later plotted to develop a line of position. If Hc is greater than Ho, then it is measured Away from the direction of the azimuth and if Ho is greater than Hc it is measured Towards the direction of the Azimuth.

Assumed Position: Taken from the assumed longitude used to find LHA and the closest whole latitude to our DR position. This is the same Latitude used to enter HO 229.

Interpolating in HO 229

Using the inputs (LHA, Lat., Dec.) look up the Hc and the Zn in the HO 229. Interpolate for Declination minutes using the formula:

> **Correction = (Dec Minutes /60)**
> **x Difference between declination**
> **and the next whole declination.**

Example

When the Latitude and Declination are the same (north or south) For LHA-12°, Latitude 15°. Declination 10° -25'

	Hc	d	Z
At 10° Dec	77°-16'	+22.8	111.7°
At 11° Dec	77°-38.8		107.5°

Since declination is actually 10°-25' its necessary to interpolate between 10° and 11°. As shown above, the difference in minutes between 77°-16' and 77°-38.8' is 22.8'. Using the formula above:

Correction to Hc= (25'/60') x 22.8 = 9.5'

> **HC = 77°-16' + 9.5'= 77°- 25.5'**

To correct for Z: 111.7° – 107.5°= 4.2°

> **Z = (25'/60') x 4.2= 1.75° (1.8)**
> **Z= 111.7° – 1.8°= 109.9°**

Plotting the Line of Position (LOP)

All the above calculations are made so a **line of position** can be put on the chart.

Step Five: Compare Ho and Hc

Find the Intercept: The difference between Ho and Hc is considered to be in miles and plotted either towards the direction of the Azimuth or away, the reciprocal, of the Azimuth based on the following rules:

> **If- Hc greater than Ho-**
> **plotted as the reciprocal of the Azimuth**
> **(Computed greater away)**

> **If- Ho greater than Hc-**
> **Plotted in the direction of the Azimuth**
> **(Ho more Towards)**

Compare the sextant sight (Ho) with the calculated altitude (Hc) to get intercept.

Intercept, difference between HC and Ho. Remember "Computed Greater Away."

> **HC - HO = Intercept**

Calculate Azimuth (Zn) from Azimuth angle (Zn) using the instructions on each page of HO 229. Remember to use correct latitude, north or south.

> **In North Latitude:**
> **LHA greater than 180°, Zn=Z**
> **LHA less than 180°, Zn= 360°- Z**

> **In South Latitude:**
> **LHA greater than 180°, Zn= 180° -Z**
> **LHA less than 180°, Zn= 180° + Z**

PLOTTING A LINE OF POSITION

The Celestial LOP of the Sun is a line perpendicular to the direction of the intercept.

Example

Intercept- 10.5 miles, Zn: 90.8° Away, Assumed Lat: 23°, Assumed Long: 47°-41.9 E

Assumed position and plotted intercept. Dotted line (intercept) is 10.5 miles long and bearing Away from (reciprocal) to 90.8°. The LOP is plotted at right angles to the intercept.

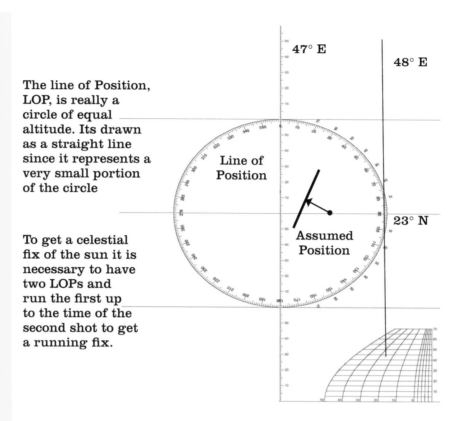

The line of Position, LOP, is really a circle of equal altitude. Its drawn as a straight line since it represents a very small portion of the circle

To get a celestial fix of the sun it is necessary to have two LOPs and run the first up to the time of the second shot to get a running fix.

Sun Line Example

This example of a Lower Limb Sun shot uses data from the 1981 Nautical Almanac, the source for all US Coast Guard questions and available online at uscg.mil/nmc. Appropriate pages are shown in the Appendix 4.

Date: August 3rd

> **DR Pos:**
> Lat   23°-12' N
> Long   47°-45' E

1. Time

Calculate time of sight at GMT (time and date). If using a chronometer remember to correct for CE, chronometer error.

> LT of Sight: 09-15-20
> ZD   -3   (47° - 45'= central meridian 45°)
> GMT   06-15-20   Date August 3rd

2. Sextant Correction

After the sight is taken (HS) correct the sight for Index Error and Height of Eye (Dip) to get Apparent Height (Ha). Find Ha correction in the Nautical Almanac to get HO, Height Observed

Index Error = 0.9 on the arc, Height of Eye- 50 ft.

Hs	52° - 53.4	
IE (+/-)	0.9'	(on the arc so -)
Dip (-)	6.9	(Height of eye- 50 ft)
Ha	51° - 45.6	
Corr.(+/-)	15.3'	(Lower limb)
Ho	52° - 00.9	

3. Nautical Almanac

Using the Almanac, determine the LHA of the body and the Declination at the GMT and date of the sight. GHA is found in the daily pages for Hr. and in the "Increments and Corrections" section for Minutes and Seconds. Declination is found next to GHA in the daily pages, d corr. is found at the bottom of the daily page and then the appropriate correction found in the Increments and Corrections section. **LHA= GHA (+EAST or –WEST) LONG**

GHA (hr)	268° -28.1	Dec.(hr)	N 17° -31.4
d 0.7			
GHA (+ m/s)	3° -50.5	d Corr	- .2
Sun GHA	272° -18.6	Dec	N 17° -31.2
A Long +	47° -41.4		
LHA	320°		

4. HO 229

Using the data above, look up the Hc and the Zn in the HO 229, enter with LHA, Assumed Latitude, and declination. Interpolate for Dec minutes Cor = (Dec Min/60) x Dif

Hc 52°-03.2	Hc Diff +/-	Z 91.6°	Z diff (+/-)
Cor. 8.2	+15.7	Cor. 0.8	-1.6 (31.2/60)X1.6= 0.8
Hc 52°-11.4			Z 90.8°

5. Comparison

Intercept, difference between HC and Ho "Computed Greater Away." Change Azimuth Angle to Azimuth.

HC 52°- 11.4'
HO 52°- 00.9
            10.5 Away
Z: 90.8° ---- Zn: 90.8° (LHA greater than 180)

To plot use:

Assumed Longitude: 47°-41.4 E
Assumed Latitude: 23° N
Intercept: 10.5 miles away
Azimuth: 90.8 (so plot AWAY from 90.8°)

CELESTIAL SIGHT OF THE MOON

"The acquisition of the knowledge of navigation
has a strange effect on the minds of men."

—Jack London

Don't fret the moon shot! With just a little extra effort, the moon
provides a celestial body that, depending on the time of the month,
can be seen either at night or during the day.

 Definitions

Upper or lower limb sights can be taken of the sun or moon. Stars
are too small.

Taking an Upper Limb: When the top of a celestial body is brought
down to the horizon and used for the sight

Taking a Lower Limb: When the bottom portion of the celestial body
is brought down to the horizon and used for the sight

Lower Limb

Upper Limb

Horizontal Parallax (HP): HP is an additional correction taken from
the daily tables and applied to find HO. It is only used in the moon
sight reduction.

See page 76 for explanation and work sheet.

CELESTIAL
WORK SHEETS

CELESTIAL WORK SHEET (SUN)

Date: _____ DR Pos: _____ Lat: _____ Long: _____

1. Time   Calculate time of sight at GMT (time and date). If using a chronometer, remember to correct for CE, chronometer error.

LT of Sight: _____   ZD: _____
Date at GMT: _____   GMT of Sight: _____

2. Sextant Correction   After the sight is taken (HS) correct the sight for Index Error and Height of Eye (Dip) to get Apparent Height (Ha). Find Ha correction in the Nautical Almanac to get HO, Height Observed

Hs
IE (+/-)
Dip (-) _____
Ha
Corr.(+/-) _____
Ho

3. Nautical Almanac   Using the Almanac, determine the LHA of the body and the Declination at the GMT time and date of the sight. GHA is found in the daily pages for Hr. and in the "Increments and Corrections" section for Minutes and Seconds. Declination is found next to GHA in the daily pages, d corr is found at the bottom of the daily page and then the appropriate correction found in the Increments and Corrections section. **LHA= GHA (+EAST –WEST) LONG**

GHA (hr)   Dec.(hr)
GHA (+ m/s) _____   d Corr _____
Sun GHA   Dec
A Long _____   A. Latitude _____
LHA

4. HO 229   Using the data above look up the Hc and the Zn in the HO 229, enter with LHA, Assumed Latitude and declination. Interpolate for Dec minutes Cor = (Dec Min/60) x Dif

Hc   Hc Diff +/-   Z   Z diff (+/-)
Cor. _____   Cor. _____
Hc   Z

5. Comparison   Intercept, difference between HC and Ho "Computed Greater Away." Change Azimuth Angle to Azimuth

HC _____ difference HO _____ Zn: _____ = Z: _____

CELESTIAL WORK SHEET (PLANET)

Date: _____ DR Pos: _____ Lat: _____ Long: _____

1. Time
Find time of sight at GMT (time and date). If using a chronometer remember to correct for CE, chronometer error.

LT of Sight: _____ ZD:_____
Date at GMT: _____ GMT of Sight: _____

2. Sextant Correction
After sight is taken (HS), correct the sight for Index Error and Height of Eye (Dip) to get Apparent Height (Ha). Find Ha correction in the Nautical Almanac to get HO,

Hs
IE (+/-)
Dip (-) _____
Ha
Corr.(+/-) _____
Ho

3. Nautical Almanac
The only difference between a planet and the sun is the v correction found at the bottom of the daily page. Add or subtract the actual correction, depending on the v sign, found in the increment pages at the rear of the Nautical Almanac. Using the Almanac, determine the LHA and the Declination. GHA is found in the daily pages for Hr. and in the "Increments and Corrections" section for Minutes and Seconds. Declination is found next to GHA in the daily pages, d corr is found at the bottom of the daily page and then the appropriate correction found in the Increments and Corrections section. **LHA= GHA (+EAST –WEST) LONG**

GHA (hr)   Dec.(hr)
GHA (+ m/s) _____   d Corr _____
V corr _____
Planet GHA   Dec
A Long _____   A. Latitude _____
LHA

4. HO 229
Using the data above look up the Hc and the Zn in the HO 229, enter with LHA, Assumed Latitude and declination. Interpolate for Dec minutes Cor = (Dec Min/60) x Dif

Hc   Hc Diff +/-   Z   Z diff (+/-)
Cor. _____   Cor. _____
Hc   Z

5. Comparison
Intercept, difference between HC and Ho "Computed Greater Away". Change Azimuth Angle to Azimuth

HC _____ difference HO _____ Zn: _____ = Z: _____

CELESTIAL WORK SHEET (STAR)

Date: _____ DR Pos: _____ Lat: _____ Long: _____

1. Time

Find time of sight at GMT (time and date). If using a chronometer remember to correct for CE, chronometer error.

LT of Sight: _____ ZD:_____
Date at GMT: _____ GMT of Sight: _____

2. Sextant Correction

After the sight is taken (HS), correct the sight for Index Error and Height of Eye (Dip) to get Apparent Height (Ha). Find Ha correction in the Nautical Almanac to get HO,

Hs
IE (+/-)
Dip (-) _____
Ha
Corr.(+/-) _____
Ho

3. Nautical Almanac

The GHA of any star is found by adding the GHA of Aires to the SHA of the star. Using the Almanac, determine the LHA and the Declination. GHA is found in the daily pages for Hr. and in the "Increments and Corrections" section for Minutes and Seconds. Declination is found next to GHA in the daily pages, d corr is found at the bottom of the daily page and then the appropriate correction found in the Increments and Corrections section. **LHA= GHA (+EAST –WEST) LONG**

GHA Aires (hr)   Dec.(hr)   d _____
GHA (+ m/s) _____ d Corr _____
SHA Star _____
GHA Star   Dec
A Long _____
LHA

4. HO 229

Using the data above, look up the Hc and the Zn in the HO 229, enter with LHA, Assumed Latitude and declination. Interpolate for Dec minutes Cor = (Dec Min/60) x Dif

Hc   Hc Diff +/- Z   Z diff (+/-)
Cor. _____   Cor. _____
Hc   Z

5. Comparison

Intercept, difference between HC and Ho "Computed Greater Away." Change Azimuth Angle to Azimuth

HC _____ difference HO _____ Z: _____ = Zn: _____

CELESTIAL WORK SHEET (MOON)

Date: _____   DR Pos: _____   Lat: _____   Long: _____

1. Time

Calculate time of sight at GMT (time and date)

LT of Sight: _____   ZD:_____
Date at GMT: _____   GMT of Sight: _____

2. Sextant Correction

The correction table for the Moon is found **at the end** of the Nautical Almanac. After the sight is taken (HS) correct the sight for Index Error and Height of Eye (dip) to get Apparent Height (Ha). Additional corrections for the moon are found at the bottom of the table.

Hs
IE (+/-)
Dip (-)_____
Ha
Alt. Corr (+/-) _____
- 30' for UL
L or U Limb correction
(HP taken from daily pages) _____
Ho

3. Nautical Almanac

Using the Almanac, determine the LHA of the body and the Declination at the GMT time and date of the sight. **LHA= GHA (+EAST –WEST) LONG**

GHA (hr)   Dec.(hr)
GHA (+ m/s) _____   d Corr _____
V correction   Dec
GHA Moon
A Long (+/-) _____
LHA

4. HO 229

Using the data above look up the Hc and the Zn in the HO 229, enter with LHA, Latitude and declination. Cor = (Dec Min/60) x Dif

Hc   Hc Diff +/-   Z   Z diff (+/-)
Cor. _____   Cor. _____
Hc   Z

5. Comparison

Find Intercept (Computed Greater Away) and change Azimuth Angle to Azimuth

HC _____ - HO _____   Z: _____   Z: _____   Zn: _____

THE NOON REPORT

Every day, on a commercial ship, the navigator prepares the Noon Report. The Report is a summary of the vessel's progress and condition from one noon to the next. The noon report contains information such as fuel onboard, fuel consumed for the last 24 hours, current weather and sea state, and the vessel's position.

Included in the report is the Slip for the past 24 hours. Below are definitions and an example of a slip calculation.

Slip: Slip is the difference between distance observed and distance computed by revolutions of the propeller. If the observed distance is greater than distance by engines slip is negative. If observed distance is less than distance by engines, slip is positive.

Why would observed be different from engine miles?

There will always be a difference between the perfect world of the engine and the medium the ship sails on. Wind and weather, along with currents, all combine to sometimes push a ship further along and sometimes hold it back from its predicted distance by engines.

Efficiency: observed speed (or dist.) / engine speed (or dist)

Efficiency = 100% -slip

Pitch: Measured in feet, is the distance the propeller would travel in one complete revolution

Nautical Mile = 6,076 feet

Miles Observed: This is the miles actually traveled from one noon report to the next, the miles by navigational observation.

First calculate the distance by engines.

Distance by Engines= This gets:	(Pitch x RPM) x 60 min. Ft/min	x 24 hrs. Ft/hr	/ 6,076= nautical miles Ft/day

CALCULATING SLIP

Example The propeller on a vessel has a diameter of 20.6 feet and a pitch of 23.4 feet. What would be the apparent slip if the vessel cruised 538 miles in a 24 hour day (observed distance) at an average RPM of 87?

Dist by Engine= ((23.4* 87) * 60 min * 24 hr.)/ 6076= 482.5 miles

Dist by Observation= 538 miles (from observation)

Now calculate the Slip:

Slip =   Dist by Engine - Dist by Observation
         Dist by Engine X 100

Slip =   482.5   -   538
         482.5   x   100 = - 11.5

APPENDICES

APPENDIX 1

Tide Table Daily Pages, Table I

BRIDGEPORT, CONN., 1983
Times and Heights of High and Low Waters

	JANUARY								FEBRUARY								MARCH						
Day	Time	Height		Day	Time	Height		Day	Time	Height		Day	Time	Height		Day	Time	Height		Day	Time	Height	
	h m	ft	m		h m	ft	m		h m	ft	m		h m	ft	m		h m	ft	m		h m	ft	m
1	0004	6.8	2.1	16	0016	6.2	1.9	1	0131	7.0	2.1	16	0057	6.6	2.0	1	0017	7.3	2.2	16	0606	-0.16	-0.2
Sa	0612	-0.8	-0.2	Su	0621	0.1	0.0	Tu	0747	-1.1	-0.3	W	0710	-0.3	-0.1	Tu	0634	-1.4	-0.4	W	1209	6.8	2.1
	1222	7.7	2.3		1227	6.8	2.1		1355	7.0	2.1		1313	6.6	2.0		1243	7.2	2.2		1821	-0.4	-0.1
	1849	-1.4	-0.4		1848	-0.3	-0.1		2014	-1.1	-0.3		1928	-0.3	-0.1		1857	-1.2	-0.4				
2	0059	6.8	2.1	17	0051	6.3	1.9	2	0224	6.9	2.1	17	0134	6.6	2.0	2	0105	7.3	2.2	17	0027	7.0	2.1
Su	0707	-0.7	-0.2	M	0659	0.2	0.1	W	0842	-0.8	-0.2	Th	0750	-0.2	-0.1	W	0725	-1.3	-0.4	Th	0644	-0.6	-0.2
	1318	7.5	2.3		1302	6.7	2.0		1450	6.6	2.0		1352	6.4	2.0		1332	6.9	2.1		1249	6.6	2.0
	1944	-1.2	-0.4		1923	-0.2	-0.1		2106	-0.7	-0.2		2006	-0.2	-0.1		1944	-0.9	-0.3		1857	-0.3	-0.1
3	0155	6.8	2.1	18	0128	6.3	1.9	3	0319	6.7	2.0	18	0216	6.6	2.0	3	0153	7.0	2.1	18	0105	7.0	2.1
M	0806	-0.6	-0.2	Tu	0736	0.2	0.1	Th	0941	-0.6	-0.2	F	0834	-0.1	0.0	Th	0815	-1.0	-0.3	F	0725	-0,5	-0.2
	1415	7.1	2.2		1341	6.5	2.0		1546	6.1	1.9		1439	6.1	1.9		1421	6.4	2.0		1332	6.4	2.0
	2040	-0.9	-0.3		2000	-0.1	0.0		2200	0.0	0.0		2048	0.0	0.0		2034	-0.5	-0.2		1937	-0.1	0.0
4	0251	6.7	2.0	19	0208	6.3	1.9	4	0414	6.5	2.0	19	0303	6.6	2.0	4	0243	6.8	2.1	19	0150	7.0	2.1
Tu	0906	-0.4	-0.1	W	0819	0.3	0.1	F	1039	-0.3	-0.1	Sa	0925	0.0	0.0	F	0908	-0.6	-0.2	Sa	0811	-0.4	-0.1
	1514	6.7	2.0		1422	6.3	1.9		1645	5.7	1.7		1530	5.9	1.8		1512	6.0	1.8		1418	6.2	1.9
	2135	-0.6	-0.2		2040	0.0	0.0		2258	0.0	0.0		2139	0.2	0.1		2125	-0.1	0.0		2023	0.1	0.0
5	0350	6.6	2.0	20	0249	6.3	1.9	5	0513	6.3	1.9	20	0357	6.5	2.0	5	0335	6.5	2.0	20	0237	6.8	2.1
W	1009	-0.3	-0.1	Th	0904	0.3	0.1	Sa	1141	-0.1	0.0	Su	1025	0.1	0.0	Sa	1003	-0.2	-0.1	Su	0904	-0.1	0.0
	1615	6.3	1.9		1509	6.1	1.9		1746	5.5	1.7		1630	5.6	1.7		1608	5.7	1.7		1512	5.9	1.8
	2234	-0.4	-0.1		2122	0.1	0.0		2356	0.2	0.1		2238	0.4	0.1		2220	0.3	0.1		2117	0.4	0.1

Subsidiary Stations, Extracts From The Tide Tables, Table II

		TABLE 2. - TIDAL DIFFERANCES AND OTHER CONSTANTS, 1983											
NO.	PLACE	POSITION				DIFFERENCES				RANGES		Mean Tide Level	
		Lat.		Long.		Time		Height		Mean	Spring		
						High Water	Low Water	High Water	Low Water				
		°	'	°	'	h. m.	h. m.	ft.	ft.	ft.	ft.	ft.	
			N		W								
	New York, East River Time meridian, 75°W					on WILLETS POINT, p.52							
1283	Lawrence Point	40	47	73	55	-0 03	+0 13	-0.7	0.0	6.4	7.6	3.2	
1285	Wolcott Avenue	40	47	73	55	-0 03	+0 13	-1.0	0.0	6.1	7.2	3.0	
						on NEW YORK, p.56							
1287	Pot Cove Astoria	40	47	73	56	+2 20	+2 29	+0.8	0.0	5.3	6.3	2.6	
1289	Hell Gate, Hallets Point	40	47	73	56	+2 00	+2 04	+0.6	0.0	5.1	6.1	2.5	
1291	Horns Hook, East 90th Street	40	47	73	57	+1 50	+1 30	+0.3	0.0	4.8	5.8	2.4	
1293	Welfare Island, north end	40	46	73	56	+1 45	+1 25	+0.3	0.0	4.8	5.8	2.4	
1295	37th Avenue, Long Island City	40	46	73	57	+1 30	+1 10	0.0	0.0	4.5	5.5	2.2	
1297	East 41st Street, New York City	40	45	73	58	+1 20	+0 56	-0.2	0.0	4.3	5.2	2.1	
1299	Hunters Point, Newtown Creek	40	44	73	57	+1 18	+0 53	-0.4	0.0	4.1	4.9	2.0	
1301	English Kills entrance, Newtown Creek	40	43	73	55	+1 30	+1 04	-0.3	0.0	4.2	5.0	2.1	
1303	East 27th Street, Bellevue Hospital	40	44	73	58	+1 08	+1 03	-0.3	0.0	4.2	5.0	2.1	
1305	East 19th Street, New York City	40	44	73	58	+1 02	+0 58	-0.4	0.0	4.1	4.9	2.0	
1307	North 3d Street, Brooklyn	40	43	73	58	+0 55	+0 42	-0.4	0.0	4.1	4.9	2.0	
1309	Williamsburg Bridge	40	43	73	58	+0 52	+0 38	-0.4	0.0	4.1	4.9	2.0	
1311	Wallabout Bay	40	42	73	59	+0 50	+0 35	-0.4	0.0	4.1	4.9	2.0	
1313	Brooklyn Bridge	40	42	73	00	+0 13	+0 07	-0.2	0.0	4.3	5.2	2.1	
	Harlem River												
1315	East 110th Street, New York City	40	47	73	56	+1 52	+1 35	+0.6	0.0	5.1	6.1	2.6	
1317	Willis Avenue Bridge	40	48	73	56	+1 47	+1 30	+0.5	0.0	5.0	6.0	2.5	
1319	Madison Avenue Bridge	40	49	73	56	+1 52	+1 35	+0.4	0.0	4.9	5.9	2.4	
1321	Central Bridge	40	50	73	56	+1 52	+1 35	+0.2	0.0	4.7	5.7	2.3	
1323	Washington Bridge	40	51	73	56	+1 52	+1 35	-0.1	0.0	4.4	5.2	2.2	
1325	University Heights Bridge	40	52	73	55	+1 40	+1 30	-0.5	0.0	4.0	4.8	2.0	
1327	Broadway Bridge	40	52	73	55	+1 20	+1 20	-0.7	0.0	3.8	3.8	1.9	
1329	Spuyten Duyvil Bridge	40	53	73	56	+1 01	+1 03	-0.9	0.0	3.6	3.6	1.8	
	Long Island Sound South Side					on WILLETS POINT, p.52							
1331	WILLETS POINT	40	48	73	47	Daily predictions				7.1	8.3	3.5	
1333	Hewlett Point	40	50	73	45	-0 03	-0 03	0.0	0.0	7.1	8.3	3.5	
1335	Port Washington, Manhasset Bay	40	50	73	42	-0 01	+0 11	+0.2	0.0	7.3	8.6	3.6	
1337	Execution Rocks	40	53	73	44	-0 06	-0 08	+0.2	0.0	7.3	8.6	3.6	
1339	Glen Cove, Hempstead Harbor	40	52	73	39	-0 11	-0 06	+0.2	0.0	7.3	8.6	3.6	
						on BRIDGEPORT, p.48							
	Oyster Bay												
1341	Oyster Bay Harbor	40	53	73	32	+0 08	+0 11	+0.6	0.0	7.3	8.4	3.6	
1343	Bayville Bridge	40	54	73	33	+0 13	+0 18	+0.7	0.0	7.4	8.5	3.7	
1345	Cold Spring Harbor	40	52	73	28	+0 08	+0 06	+0.7	0.0	7.4	8.5	3.7	
1347	Eatons Neck Point	40	57	73	24	+0 03	+0 06	+0.4	0.0	7.1	8.2	3.6	
1349	Lloyd Harbor entrance, Huntington Bay	40	55	73	26	+0 03	+0 01	+0.7	0.0	7.4	8.5	3.7	
1351	Northport, Northport Bay	40	54	73	21	+0 03	+0 06	+0.6	0.0	7.3	8.4	3.6	
1353	Nisssequogue River entrance	40	54	73	14	-0 03	-0 06	+0.3	0.0	7.0	8.0	3.5	
1355	Stony Brook, Smithtown Bay	40	55	73	09	+0 08	+0 08	-0.6	0.0	6.1	7.0	3.0	
1357	Stratford Shoal	41	04	73	06	-0 05	-0 09	-0.1	0.0	6.6	7.6	3.3	
1359	Port Jefferson Harbor entrance	40	58	73	05	+0 03	-0 01	-0.1	0.0	6.6	7.6	3.3	
1361	Port Jefferson	40	57	73	05	+0 06	+0 03	-0.1	0.0	6.6	7.6	3.3	
1363	Setauket Harbor	40	57	73	06	+0 04	+0 09	0.0	0.0	6.7	7.7	3.3	
1365	Conscience Bay entrance (Narrows)	40	58	73	07	+0 02	+0 02	0.0	0.0	6.7	7.7	3.3	
1367	Mount Sinai Harbor	40	58	73	02	+0 05	+0 16	-0.7	0.0	6.0	6.9	3.0	
1369	Herod Point	40	58	72	50	-0 07	-0 16	-0.8	0.0	5.9	6.8	2.9	
1370	Northville	40	59	72	39	-0 02	-0 05	-1.3	0.0	5.4	6.2	2.7	
1371	Mattituck Inlet	41	01	72	34	+0 05	-0 06	-1.5	0.0	5.2	6.0	2.6	
1373	Horton Point	41	05	72	27	-0 20	-0 35	*0.60	*0.60	4.0	4.6	2.0	
1374	Hashamount Beach	41	06	72	24	+0 04	-0 15	*0.63	*0.63	4.2	4.8	2.1	
1375	Truman Beach	41	08	72	19	-0 42	-0 52	*0.51	*0.51	3.4	3.9	1.7	

Height of Tide At Any Time, Table III

	TIME FROM THE NEAREST HIGH WATER OR LOW WATER														
h. m.	h. m.	h. m.	h. m.	h. m.	h. m.	h. m.	h. m.	h. m.	h. m.	h. m.	h. m.	h. m.	h. m.	h. m.	h. m.
4 00	0 08	0 16	0 24	0 32	0 40	0 48	0 56	1 04	1 12	1 20	1 28	1 36	1 44	1 52	2 00
4 20	0 09	0 17	0 26	0 35	0 43	0 52	1 01	1 09	1 18	1 27	1 35	1 44	1 53	2 01	2 10
4 40	0 09	0 19	0 28	0 37	0 47	0 56	1 05	1 15	1 24	1 33	1 43	1 52	2 01	2 11	2 20
5 00	0 10	0 20	0 30	0 40	0 50	1 00	1 10	1 20	1 30	1 40	1 50	2 00	2 10	2 20	2 30
5 20	0 11	0 21	0 32	0 43	0 53	1 04	1 15	1 25	1 36	1 47	1 57	2 08	2 19	2 29	2 40
5 40	0 11	0 23	0 34	0 45	0 57	1 08	1 19	1 31	1 42	1 53	2 05	2 16	2 27	2 39	2 50
6 00	0 12	0 24	0 36	0 48	1 00	1 12	1 24	1 36	1 48	2 00	2 12	2 24	2 36	2 48	3 00
6 20	0 13	0 25	0 38	0 51	1 03	1 16	1 29	1 41	1 54	2 07	2 19	2 32	2 45	2 57	3 10
6 40	0 13	0 27	0 40	0 53	1 07	1 20	1 33	1 47	2 00	2 13	2 27	2 40	2 53	3 07	3 20
7 00	0 14	0 28	0 42	0 56	1 10	1 24	1 38	1 52	2 06	2 20	2 34	2 48	3 02	3 16	3 30
7 20	0 15	0 29	0 44	0 59	1 13	1 28	1 43	1 57	2 12	2 27	2 41	2 56	3 11	3 25	3 40
7 40	0 15	0 31	0 46	1 01	1 17	1 32	1 47	2 03	2 18	2 33	2 49	3 04	3 19	3 35	3 50
8 00	0 16	0 32	0 48	1 04	1 20	1 36	1 52	2 08	2 24	2 40	2 56	3 12	3 28	3 44	4 00
8 20	0 17	0 33	0 50	1 07	1 23	1 40	1 57	2 13	2 30	2 47	3 03	3 20	3 37	3 53	4 10
8 40	0 17	0 35	0 52	1 09	1 27	1 44	2 01	2 19	2 36	2 53	3 11	3 28	3 45	4 03	4 20
9 00	0 18	0 36	0 54	1 12	1 30	1 48	2 06	2 24	2 42	3 00	3 18	3 30	3 54	4 12	4 30
9 20	0 19	0 37	0 56	1 15	1 33	1 52	2 11	2 29	2 48	3 07	3 25	3 44	4 03	4 21	4 40
9 40	0 19	0 39	0 58	1 17	1 37	1 56	2 15	2 35	2 54	3 13	3 33	3 52	4 11	4 31	4 50
10 00	0 20	0 40	1 00	1 20	1 40	2 00	2 20	2 40	3 00	3 20	3 40	4 00	4 20	4 40	5 00
10 20	0 21	0 41	1 02	1 23	1 43	2 04	2 25	2 45	3 06	3 27	3 47	4 08	4 29	4 49	5 10
10 40	0 21	0 43	1 04	1 25	1 47	2 08	2 29	2 51	3 12	3 33	3 55	4 16	4 37	4 59	5 20

Left of table, vertical: Duration of rise or fall, see footnote

	CORRECTION TO HEIGHT														
Ft.	Ft.	Ft.	Ft.	Ft.	Ft.	Ft.	Ft.	Ft.	Ft.	Ft.	Ft.	Ft.	Ft.	Ft.	Ft.
0.5	0.0	0.0	0.0	0.0	0.0	0.0	0.1	0.1	0.1	0.1	0.1	0.2	0.2	0.2	0.2
1.0	0.0	0.0	0.0	0.0	0.1	0.1	0.1	0.2	0.2	0.2	0.3	0.3	0.4	0.4	0.5
1.5	0.0	0.0	0.0	0.1	0.1	0.1	0.2	0.2	0.3	0.4	0.4	0.5	0.6	0.7	0.8
2.0	0.0	0.0	0.0	0.1	0.1	0.2	0.3	0.3	0.4	0.5	0.6	0.7	0.8	0.9	1.0
2.5	0.0	0.0	0.1	0.1	0.2	0.2	0.3	0.4	0.5	0.6	0.7	0.9	1.0	1.1	1.2
3.0	0.0	0.0	0.1	0.1	0.2	0.3	0.4	0.5	0.6	0.8	0.9	1.0	1.2	1.3	1.5
3.5	0.0	0.0	0.1	0.2	0.2	0.3	0.4	0.6	0.7	0.9	1.0	1.2	1.4	1.6	1.8
4.0	0.0	0.0	0.1	0.2	0.3	0.4	0.5	0.7	0.8	1.0	1.2	1.4	1.6	1.8	2.0
4.5	0.0	0.0	0.1	0.2	0.3	0.4	0.6	0.7	0.9	1.1	1.3	1.6	1.8	2.0	2.2
5.0	0.0	0.1	0.1	0.2	0.3	0.5	0.6	0.8	1.0	1.2	1.5	1.7	2.0	2.2	2.5
5.5	0.0	0.1	0.1	0.2	0.4	0.5	0.7	0.9	1.1	1.4	1.6	1.9	2.2	2.5	2.8
6.0	0.0	0.1	0.1	0.3	0.4	0.6	0.8	1.0	1.2	1.5	1.8	2.1	2.4	2.7	3.0
6.5	0.0	0.1	0.2	0.3	0.4	0.6	0.8	11	1.3	1.6	1.9	2.2	2.6	2.9	3.2
7.0	0.0	0.1	0.2	0.3	0.5	0.7	0.9	1.2	1.4	1.8	2.1	2.4	2.8	3.1	3.5
7.5	0.0	0.1	0.2	0.3	0.5	0.7	1.0	1.2	1.5	1.9	2.2	2.6	3.0	3.4	3.8
8.0	0.0	0.1	0.2	0.3	0.5	0.8	1.0	1.3	1.6	2.0	2.4	2.8	3.2	3.6	4.0
8.5	0.0	0.1	0.2	0.4	0.6	0.8	1.1	1.4	1.8	2.1	2.5	2.9	3.4	3.8	4.2
9.0	0.0	0.1	0.2	0.4	0.6	0.9	1.2	1.5	1.9	2.2	2.7	3.1	3.6	4.0	4.5
9.5	0.0	0.1	0.2	0.4	0.6	0.9	1.2	1.6	2.0	2.4	2.8	3.3	3.8	4.3	4.8
10.0	0.0	0.1	0.2	0.4	0.7	1.0	1.3	1.7	2.1	2.5	3.0	3.5	4.0	4.5	5.0
10.5	0.0	0.1	0.3	0.5	0.7	1.0	1.3	1.7	2.2	2.6	3.1	3.6	4.2	4.7	5.2
11.0	0.0	0.1	0.3	0.5	0.7	1.1	1.4	1.8	2.3	2.8	3.3	3.8	4.4	4.9	5.5
11.5	0.0	0.1	0.3	0.5	0.8	1.1	1.5	1.9	2.4	2.9	3.4	4.0	4.6	5.1	5.8
12.0	0.0	0.1	0.3	0.5	0.8	1.1	1.5	2.0	2.5	3.0	3.6	4.1	4.8	5.4	6.0
12.5	0.0	0.1	0.3	0.5	0.8	1.2	1.6	2.1	2.6	3.1	3.7	4.3	5.0	5.6	6.2
13.0	0.0	0.1	0.3	0.6	0.9	1.2	1.7	2.2	2.7	3.2	3.9	4.5	5.1	5.8	6.5
13.5	0.0	0.1	0.3	0.6	0.9	1.3	1.7	2.2	2.8	34	4.0	4.7	5.3	6.0	6.8
14.0	0.0	0.2	0.3	0.6	0.9	1.3	1.8	2.3	2.9	3.5	4.2	4.8	5.5	6.3	7.0
14.5	0.0	0.2	0.4	0.6	1.0	1.4	1.9	2.4	3.0	3.6	4.3	5.0	5.7	6.5	7.2
15.0	0.0	0.2	0.4	0.6	1.0	1.4	1.9	2.5	3.1	3.8	4.4	5.2	5.9	6.7	7.5
15.5	0.0	0.2	0.4	0.7	1.0.	1.5	2.0	2.6	3.2	3.9	4.6	5.4	6.1	6.9	7.8
16.0	0.0	0.2	0.4	0.7	1.1	1.5	2.1	2.6	3.3	4.0	4.7	5.5	6.3	7.2	8.0
16.5	0.0	0.2	0.4	0.7	1.1	1.6	2.1	2.7	3.4	4.1	4.9	5.7	6.5	7.4	8.2
17.0	0.0	0.2	0.4	0.7	1.1	1.6	2.2	2.8	3.5	4.2	5.0	5.9	6.7	7.6	8.5
17.5	0.0	0.2	0.4	0.8	1.2	1.7	2.2	2.9	3.6	4.4	5.2	6.0	6.9	7.8	8.8
18.0	0.0	0.2	0.4	0.8	1.2	1.7	2.3	3.0	3.7	4.5	5.3	6.2	7.1	8.1	9.0
18.5	0.1	0.2	0.5	0.8	1.2	1.8	2.4	3.1	3.8	4.6	5.5	6.4	7.3	8.3	9.2
19.0	0.1	0.2	0.5	0.8	1.3	1.8	2.4	3.1	3.9	4.8	5.6	6.6	7.5	8.5	9.5
19.5	0.1	0.2	0.5	0.8	1.3	1.9	2.5	3.2	4.0	4.9	5.8	6.7	7.7	8.7	9.8
20.0	0.1	0.2	0.5	0.9	1.3	1.9	2.6	3.3	4.1	5.0	5.9	6.9	7.9	9.0	10.0

Left of table, vertical: Range of tide, see footnote

Obtain from the predictions the high water and lower water, one of which is before and the other after the time for which the height is required. The difference between the times of occurrence of these tides is the duration of rise or fall, and the difference between their heights is the range of tide for the above table. Find the difference between the nearest high or low water and the time for which height is required.

Enter the table with the duration of rise or fall, printed in heavy-faced type, which most nearly agrees withthe acutal value, and on that horizontal line find the time from the nearest high or low in the column directly below, on the line with the range of tide.

When the nearest tied is high water, subtract the correctio.

When the nearest ties is low water, add the correction

APPENDIX 2

Tidal Current Daily Pages, Table I

POLLOCK RIP CHANNEL, MASSACHUSETTS.1983
F-Flood, Dir. 035° True   E-Ebb, Dir. 225° True

JULY

Day	Slack Water Time h.m.	Maximum Current Time h.m.	Vel. knots
1 F	0116	0356	1.7E
	0702	1029	2.0F
	1352	1628	1.6E
	1940	2251	1.7F
2 Sa	0205	0441	1.6E
	0749	1114	2.0F
	1438	1717	1.7E
	2028	2342	1.7F
3 Su	0256	0533	1.6E
	0838	1200	1.9F
	1526	1804	1.7E
	2116		
4 M		0031	1.7F
	0348	0624	1.6E
	0929	1251	1.8F
	1614	1853	1.7E
	2206		
5 Tu		0122	1.7F
	0442	0715	1.5E
	1022	1343	1.8F
	1703	1943	1.7E
	2256		
6 W		0218	1.8F
	0535	0808	1.5E
	1115	1434	1.8F
	1752	2032	1.7E
	2345		
7 Th		0307	1.9F
	0627	0901	1.6E
	1208	1522	1.8F
	1840	2123	1.8E
8 F	0033	0356	2.0F
	0719	0955	1.6E
	1301	1616	1.8F
	1928	2210	1.8E
9 Sa	0122	0447	2.1F
	0810	1044	1.7E
	1352	1705	1.8F
	2016	2301	1.9E
10 Su	0211	0535	2.2F
	0900	1137	1.8E
	1444	1754	1.9F
	2105	2351	2.0E
11 M	0300	0623	2.3F
	0950	1228	1.8E
	1535	1845	1.9F
	2155		
12 Tu		0042	2.0E
	0351	0715	2.3F
	1041	1319	1.9E
	1628	1938	1.9F
	2247		
13 W		0135	2.0E
	0444	0810	2.3F
	1133	1411	1.9E
	1722	2033	1.9F
	2342		
14 Th		0135	2.0E
	0444	0810	2.3F
	1133	1411	1.9E
	1722	2033	1.9F
	2342		
15 F	0040	0325	1.9E
	0635	1006	2.2F
	1323	1603	1.8E
	1916	2235	1.9F

Day	Slack Water Time h.m.	Maximum Current Time h.m.	Vel. knots
16 Sa	0140	0425	1.8E
	0735	1107	2.1F
	1420	1704	1.7E
	2016	2342	1.9F
17 Su	0243	0530	1.7E
	0838	1212	2.0F
	1519	1807	1.7E
	2118		
18 M		0048	1.9F
	0348	0636	1.6E
	0943	1321	2.0F
	1618	191	1.7E
	2220		
19 Tu		0155	2.0F
	0453	0746	1.5E
	1047	1423	1.9F
	1717	2015	1.7E
	2320		
20 W		0256	2.0F
	0556	0851	1.5E
	1150	1522	1.9F
	1813	2115	1.7E
21 Th	0017	0354	2.1F
	0654	0952	1.6E
	1248	1617	1.9F
	1905	2208	1.7E
22 F	0109	0445	2.2F
	0747	1045	1.6E
	1341	1708	1.9F
	1954	2256	1.7E
23 Sa	0156	0534	2.2F
	0835	1131	1.6E
	1428	1751	1.9F
	2039	2338	1.7E
24 Su	0239	0617	2.2F
	0919	1210	1.6E
	1510	1833	1.8F
	2120		
25 M		0016	1.7E
	0318	0656	2.2F
	0959	1247	1.6E
	1548	1910	1.8F
	2200		
26 Tu		0049	1.8E
	0355	0731	2.2F
	1037	1320	1.7E
	1624	1945	1.8F
	2239		
27 W		0124	1.8E
	0431	0803	2.2F
	1114	1354	1.7E
	1701	2016	1.8F
	2318		
28 Th		0201	1.8E
	0508	0836	2.1F
	1151	1429	1.7E
	2120	2050	1.8F
	2358		
29 F		0201	1.8E
	0508	0836	2.1F
	1151	1429	1.7E
	2120	2050	1.8F
	2358		
30 Sa	0041	0318	1.8E
	0626	0944	2.1F
	1312	1547	1.8E
	1857	2206	1.8F
31 Su	0126	0403	1.7E
	0710	1026	2.0F
	1355	1632	1.7E
	1941	2251	1.8F

AUGUST

Day	Slack Water Time h.m.	Maximum Current Time h.m.	Vel. knots
1 M	0215	0452	1.7E
	0756	1111	1.9F
	1442	1720	1.7E
	2029	2340	1.8F
2 Tu	0307	0543	1.6E
	0847	1202	1.8F
	1531	1809	1.7E
	2119		
3 W		0034	1.8F
	0403	0638	1.6E
	0942	1257	1.7
	1623	1902	1.6E
	2213		
4 Th		0131	1.8F
	0501	0734	1.5E
	1041	1352	1.6F
	1717	1957	1.6E
	2309		
5 F		0234	1.8F
	0559	0831	1.5E
	1140	1454	1.6F
	1811	2052	1.7E
6 Sa	0005	0332	1.9F
	0656	0931	1.5E
	1239	1555	1.7F
	1905	2148	1.8E
7 Su	0100	0430	2.1F
	0751	1027	1.6
	1336	1651	1.8F
	1958	2243	1.9E
8 M	0154	0525	2.2F
	0843	1121	1.8E
	1430	1744	1.9F
	2050	2336	2.0E
9 Tu	0247	0615	2.3F
	0934	1214	1.9E
	1522	1836	2.0F
	2141		
10 W		0029	2.1E
	0339	0706	2.4F
	1024	1305	1.9E
	1613	1928	2.1F
	2233		
11 Th		0120	2.1E
	0431	0757	2.4F
	1114	1354	2.0E
	1704	2020	2.1F
	2326		
12 W		0214	2.1E
	0523	0214	2.3F
	1205	1448	1.9E
	1756	2114	2.1F
13 Sa	0021	0305	2.0E
	0617	0943	2.2F
	1257	1540	1.9E
	1850	2212	2.0F
14 Su	0119	0403	1.8E
	0714	1044	2.1F
	1352	1636	1.8E
	1947	2314	2.0F
15 M	0220	0504	1.7E
	0814	1145	1.9F
	1449	1737	1.7E
	2046		

Day	Slack Water Time h.m.	Maximum Current Time h.m.	Vel. knots
16 Tu		0021	1.9F
	0232	0612	1.5E
	0917	1251	1.8F
	1548	1841	1.6E
	2149		
17 W		0128	1.9F
	0428	0721	1.5E
	1022	1356	1.8F
	1648	1949	1.5E
	2251		
18 Th		0230	2.0F
	0531	0828	1.4E
	1126	1457	1.8F
	1746	2048	1.6F
	2349		
19 F		0329	2.1F
	0630	0928	1.5E
	1225	1553	1.8F
	1841	2145	1.6E
20 Sa	0043	0422	2.1F
	0723	1021	1.6E
	1317	1644	1.9F
	1930	2230	1.7E
21 Su	0131	0507	2.2F
	0809	1106	1.6E
	1403	1727	1.9F
	2015	2315	1.7E
22 M	0214	0550	2.2F
	0851	1145	1.7E
	1444	1808	1.9F
	2056	2351	1.8E
23 Tu	0253	0628	2.2F
	0929	1220	1.7E
	1520	1843	1.9F
	2135		
24 W		0025	1.8E
	0329	0701	2.2F
	1005	1251	1.8E
	1554	1915	1.9F
	2122		
25 Th		0056	1.9E
	0403	0730	2.2F
	1041	1321	1.8E
	1628	1944	2.0F
26 F		0131	1.9E
	0438	0800	2.2F
	1116	1354	1.9E
	1702	2013	2.0F
	2327		
27 Sa		0208	1.9E
	0514	0829	2.1F
	1153	1429	1.9E
	1737	2048	2.0F
28 Su		0245	1.9E
	0552	0906	2.1F
	1232	1509	1.8E
	1816	2127	1.9F
29 M	0050	0330	1.8E
	0633	0945	2.0F
	1314	1552	1.8E
	1858	2206	1.9F
30 Tu	0139	0415	1.7E
	0720	1028	1.8F
	1400	1639	1.7E
	1945	2258	1.8F
31 W	02332	0508	1.6E
	0812	1121	1.7F
	1452	1732	1.6E
	2038	2355	1.8F

Extracts From The Tidal Current Tables, Subsidiary Stations, Table II

NO.	PLACE	METER DEPTH	POSITION		TIME DIFFERENCES				SPEED RATIOS		AVERAGE SPEEDS AND DIRECTIONS			
			Lat.	Long.	Min. before Flood	Flood	Min. Before Ebb	Ebb	Flood	Ebb	Minimum before Flood	Maximum Flood	Minimum before Ebb	Maximum Ebb
		ft	° '	° '	h. m.	h. m.	h. m.	h. m.			knots deg.	knots deg.	knots deg.	knots deg.
	CAPE COD BAY Time meridian, 75°w		N	W	on BOSTON HARBOR, 9.16									
1231	Race Point, 7 miles north of		42 11	70 16	-0 01	-0 01	-0 01	-0 01	1.4	1.2	0.0 --	1.5 290	0.0 --	1.5 --
1236	Race Point, 1 mile northwest of		42 05	70 15	-0 06	-0 06	-0 06	-0 06	0.9	0.8	0.0 --	1.0 226	0.0 --	0.9 061
1241	Provincetown harbor		42 03	70 10	+0 04	+0 04	+0 04	+0 04	0.5	0.3	0.0 --	0.6 315	0.0 --	0.4 135
1246	Wellfleet Harbor		41 54	70 03	+0 09	+0 09	+0 09	+0 09	0.6	0.4	0.0 --	0.7 020	0.0 --	0.5 200
1251	Barnstable Harbor		41 43.6	70 16.4	+0 19	+0 58	+0 22	+0 29	1.1	1.2	0.0 --	1.2 192	0.0 --	1.4 004
1256	Sandwich Harbor		41 46	70 29	Current weak and variable									
	Cape Cod Canal (see Index)		-- --	-- --	-- --	-- --	-- --	-- --	-- --		-- --	-- --	-- --	-- --
1261	Safamore Beach		41 48	70 31	Current weak and variable									
1266	Ellisville Harbor, 1 mile east of		41 51	70 30	+0 14	+0 14	+0 14	+0 14	0.3	0.2	0.0 --	0.3 200	0.0 --	0.3 020
1271	Manomet Point		41 56	70 32	+0 04	+0 04	+0 04	+0 04	1.0	0.7	0.0 --	1.1 155	0.0 --	0.9 010
1276	Gurnet Point, 1 mile east of		42 00	70 35	-0 06	-0 06	-0 06	-0 06	1.3	0.8	0.0 --	1.4 250	0.0 --	1.0 --
1281	Plymouth Harbor		41 58	70 39	+0 04	+0 04	+0 04	+0 04	1.5	0.3	0.0 --	0.5 245	0.0 --	0.4 010
1286	Farnham Rock, 1 mile east of		42 06	70 35	-0 21	-0 21	-0 21	-0 21	1.0	0.8	0.0 --	1.1 180	0.0 --	0.9 010
	MASSACHUSETTS COAST-Continued				on POLLACK RIP CHANNEL. P.28									
1291	Nauset Beach Light, 5 miles northeast of		41 56	69 54	See table 5									
1296	Georges Bank and vicinity		-- --	-- --	See table 5				1.4	1.2	0.0 --	1.5 290	0.0 --	1.5 --
1301	Davis Bank		-- --	-- --	See table 5				1.4	1.2	0.0 --	1.5 290	0.0 --	1.5 --
1306	Monomoy Point, 23 miles east of		41 35	69 30	See table 5				1.4	1.2	0.0 --	1.5 290	0.0 --	1.5 --
1311	Nantucket Shoals		40 37	69 37	See table 5				1.4	1.2	0.0 --	1.5 290	0.0 --	1.5 --
1316	Nantucket Island, 28 miles east of		41 20	69 21	See table 5									
1321	Old Man Shoal, Nantucket Shoals		41 13.6	69 59.0	+1 23	+1 03	+1 17	+1 14						
1326	Miacomet Pond, 3.0 miles SSE of		41 11.4	70 05.8	+2 19	+2 03	+2 22	+2 16						
1331	Tuckernuck Island, 4.2 miles SSW of		41 13.57	70 16.90	+4 08	+3 13	+2 17	+3 56						
1336	Martha's Vineyard, 1.4 miles S of <1>		41 19.50	70 39.90	- - -	-2 53	- - -	-2 47	0.1	0.1	0.0 --	0.3 230	0.0 --	0.3 095
	NANTUCKET SOUND ENTRANCE													
1341	Pollock Rip Channel, east end		41 33.9	69 55.4	-0 14	-0 39	-0 23	-0 38	1.0	1.1	0.0 --	2.0 053	0.0 --	1.8 212
1346	POLLOCK RIP CHANNEL (Butler Hole)		41 33	69 59	Daily predictions						0.0 --	2.0 037	0.0 --	1.8 226
1351	Great Round Shoal Channel		-- --	-- --	See table 5									
	NANTUCKET SOUND ENTRANCE													
1356	Monomoy Pt., channel 0.2 mile west of		41 33.0	70 01.3	0 00	+0 39	+0 18	-0 23	0.8	1.2	0.0 --	1.7 170	0.0 --	2.0 346
1361	Chatham Roads		40 38.6	70 01.7	Current weak and variable									
1366	Stage Harbor, west of Morris Island		41 39.4	69 58.5	+3 07	+1 29	+2 24	+4 28	0.3	0.6	0.0 --	0.5 335	0.0 --	1.0 144
1371	Dennis Port, 2.2 miles south of		41 37.0	70 06.9	+1 28	+0 52	+0 27	+1 04	1.0	1.1	0.0 --	2.0 037	0.0 --	1.8 212
1376	Monomoy Point, 6 miles west of		41 33.5	70 09.0	+1 22	+1 52	+1 09	+1 22	1.0	1.1	0.0 --	2.0 053	0.0 --	1.8 226
1381	Handkerchief Lighted Whistle Booy "H"		41 29.3	70 04.0	+1 08	+1 10	+0 49	+0 59	1.0	1.1	0.0 --	2.0 037	0.0 --	1.8 212
1386	Halfmoon Shoal, 1.9 miles northeast of		41 29.05	70 11.55	+1 42	+1 49	+1 24	+1 44	1.0	1.1	0.0 --	2.0 037	0.0 --	1.8 226
1391	Halfmoon Shoal, 3.5 miles east of		41 28.1	70 09.2	+1 13	+1 23	+1 06	+1 11	1.0	1.1	0.0 --	2.0 037	0.0 --	1.8 226
1396	Great Point, 0.5 mile west of		41 23.6	70 03.7	+0 25	+1 37	+1 13	+0 33	1.0	1.1	0.0 --	2.0 037	0.0 --	1.8 226
1401	Great Point, 3 miles west of		41 23.4	70 06.8	+1 15	+1 23	+0 51	+1 08	1.0	1.1	0.0 --	2.0 037	0.0 --	1.8 226
1406	Tuckernuck Shoal, off east end		41 24.3	70 10.4	+1 22	+1 34	+1 09	+1 10	1.0	1.1	0.0 --	2.0 037	0.0 --	1.8 226

Velocity Of Current at any Time, Table III

TABLE A

Interval between slack and desired time (h. m.)	Interval between slack and maximum current													
	h. m. 1 20	h. m. 1 40	h. m. 2 00	h. m. 2 20	h. m. 2 40	h. m. 3 00	h. m. 3 20	h. m. 3 40	h. m. 4 00	h. m. 4 20	h. m. 4 40	h. m. 5 00	h. m. 5 20	h. m. 5 40
	f.	f.	f.	f.	f.	f.	f.	f.	f.	f.	f.	f.	f.	f.
0 20	0.4	0.3	0.3	0.2	0.2	0.2	0.2	0.1	0.1	0.1	0.1	0.1	0.1	0.1
0 40	0.7	0.6	0.5	0.4	0.4	0.3	0.3	0.3	0.3	0.2	0.2	0.2	0.2	0.2
1 00	0.9	0.8	0.7	0.6	0.6	0.5	0.5	0.4	0.4	0.4	0.3	0.3	0.3	0.3
1 20	1.0	1.0	.09	0.8	0.7	0.6	0.6	0.5	0.5	0.5	0.4	0.4	0.4	0.4
1 40	------	1.0	1.0	0.9	0.8	0.8	0.7	0.7	0.6	0.6	0.5	0.5	0.5	0.4
2 00	------	------	1.0	1.0	0.9	0.9	0.8	0.8	0.7	0.7	0.6	0.6	0.6	0.5
2 20	------	------	------	1.0	1.0	0.9	0.9	0.8	0.8	0.7	0.7	0.7	0.6	0.6
2 40	------	------	------	------	1.0	1.0	1.0	0.9	0.9	0.8	0.8	0.7	0.7	0.07
3 00	------	------	------	------	------	1.0	1.0	1.0	0.9	0.9	0.8	.08	0.8	0.7
3 20	------	------	------	------	------	------	1.0	1.0	1.0	0.9	0.9	0.9	0.8	0.8
3 40	------	------	------	------	------	------	------	1.0	1.0	1.0	0.9	0.9	0.9	.09
4 00	------	------	------	------	------	------	------	------	1.0	1.0	1.0	1.0	0.9	0.9
4 20	------	------	------	------	------	------	------	------	------	1.0	1.0	1.0	1.0	0.9
4 40	------	------	------	------	------	------	------	------	------	------	1.0	1.0	1.0	1.0
5 00	------	------	------	------	------	------	------	------	------	------	------	1.0	1.0	1.0
5 20	------	------	------	------	------	------	------	------	------	------	------	------	1.0	1.0
5 40	------	------	------	------	------	------	------	------	------	------	------	------	------	1.0

TABLE B

Interval between slack and desired time (h. m.)	Interval between slack and maximum current													
	h. m. 1 20	h. m. 1 40	h. m. 2 00	h. m. 2 20	h. m. 2 40	h. m. 3 00	h. m. 3 20	h. m. 3 40	h. m. 4 00	h. m. 4 20	h. m. 4 40	h. m. 5 00	h. m. 5 20	h. m. 5 40
	f.	f.	f.	f.	f.	f.	f.	f.	f.	f.	f.	f.	f.	f.
0 20	0.5	0.4	0.4	0.3	0.3	0.3	0.3	0.3	0.2	0.2	0.2	0.2	0.2	0.2
0 40	0.5	0.7	0.6	0.5	0.5	0.5	0.4	0.4	0.4	0.4	0.3	0.3	0.3	0.3
1 00	0.9	0.8	0.8	0.7	0.7	0.6	0.6	0.5	0.5	0.5	0.4	0.4	0.4	0.4
1 20	1.0	1.0	0.9	0.8	0.8	0.7	0.7	0.6	0.6	0.6	0.5	0.5	0.5	0.5
1 40	------	1.0	1.0	0.9	0.9	0.8	0.8	0.7	0.7	0.7	0.6	0.6	0.6	0.6
2 00	------	------	1.0	1.0	0.9	0.9	0.9	0.8	0.8	0.7	0.7	0.7	0.7	0.6
2 20	------	------	------	1.0	1.0	1.0	0.9	0.9	0.8	0.8	0.8	0.7	0.7	0.7
2 40	------	------	------	------	1.0	1.0	1.0	0.9	0.9	0.9	0.8	0.8	0.8	0.7
3 00	------	------	------	------	------	1.0	1.0	1.0	0.9	0.9	0.9	0.8	0.8	0.8
3 20	------	------	------	------	------	------	1.0	1.0	1.0	1.0	0.9	0.9	0.9	0.8
3 40	------	------	------	------	------	------	------	1.0	1.0	1.0	1.0	0.9	0.9	0.9
4 00	------	------	------	------	------	------	------	------	1.0	1.0	1.0	1.0	0.9	0.9
4 20	------	------	------	------	------	------	------	------	------	1.0	1.0	1.0	1.0	0.9
4 40	------	------	------	------	------	------	------	------	------	------	1.0	1.0	1.0	1.0
5 00	------	------	------	------	------	------	------	------	------	------	------	1.0	1.0	1.0
5 20	------	------	------	------	------	------	------	------	------	------	------	------	1.0	1.0
5 40	------	------	------	------	------	------	------	------	------	------	------	------	------	1.0

Use table A for all places except those listed for table B.
Use table B for Cape Cod Canal, Hell Gate, Chesapeake and Delaware Canal and alll stations in table 2 which are referred to them.

1. From predictions find the time of slack water and the time and velocity of maximum current (flood or ebb), one of which is immediately before and the other after the time for which the velocity is desired.
2. Find the interval of time between the above slack and maximum current, and enter the top of table A or B with the interval which mostly agrees with this value.
3. Find the interval of time between the above slack and the time desired, and enter the side of table A or B with the interval which most nearly agrees with this value.
4. Find, in the table, the factor corresponding to the above two intervals., and multiply the maximum velocity by this factor. The result will be the approximate velocity at the time desired.

APPENDIX 3: COMPASS

Deviation Table Worksheet

Vessel Name:			Date:			
Gyro	Gyro Error	True	Variation	Magnetic	Deviation	PSC
000°						
015°						
030°						
045°						
060°						
075°						
090°						
105°						
120°						
135°						
150°						
175°						
180°						
195°						
210°						
225°						
240°						
255°						
270°						
285°						
300°						
315°						
330°						
345°						

Directions: To make a deviation table, steady the ship on the gyro heading every fifteen degrees and note the Magnetic Compass (PSC) course. Find the magnetic heading using rules below. The difference between PSC and Magnetic is the deviation on that heading. If PSC is greater, error is west. If PSC is less error is east.

Gyro Error: Add East, Subtract West to get True

Variation: Add West, Subtract East to get Magnetic Heading

Deviation Table

Vessel Name:															
Date:															
Mag. Heading:	Deviation West								Deviation East						
000°	7°	6°	5°	4°	3°	2°	1°	0°	1°	2°	3°	4°	5°	6°	7°
015°															
030°															
045°															
060°															
075°															
090°															
105°															
120°															
135°															
150°															
175°															
180°															
195°															
210°															
225°															
240°															
255°															
270°															
285°															
300°															
315°															
330°															
345°															

Directions: Plot results of Deviation Work Sheet. The results should resemble a vertical sign curve.

APPENDIX 4: EXTRACTS FROM NAUTICAL ALMANAC AND H.O. 229

SUN and MOON

G.M.T.	SUN G.H.A.	SUN Dec.	MOON G.H.A.	v	Dec.	d	H.P.
18 00	176 29.8	S11 44.1	7 18.2	10.5	N16 04.4	7.2	56.6
01	191 29.8	43.2	21 47.7	10.6	15 57.2	7.2	56.5
02	206 29.9	42.4	36 17.3	10.6	15 50.0	7.4	56.5
03	221 30.0 ··	41.5	50 46.9	10.7	15 42.6	7.4	56.5
04	236 30.0	40.6	65 16.6	10.7	15 35.2	7.5	56.5
05	251 30.1	39.7	79 46.3	10.8	15 27.7	7.5	56.5
06	266 30.1	S11 38.8	94 16.1	10.9	N15 20.2	7.6	56.4
07	281 30.2	38.0	108 46.0	10.9	15 12.6	7.7	56.4
W 08	296 30.2	37.1	123 15.9	11.0	15 04.9	7.8	56.4
E 09	311 30.3 ··	36.2	137 45.9	11.1	14 57.1	7.9	56.4
D 10	326 30.3	35.3	152 16.0	11.1	14 49.2	7.9	56.3
N 11	341 30.4	34.4	166 46.1	11.2	14 41.3	8.0	56.3
E 12	356 30.4	S11 33.5	181 16.3	11.2	N14 33.3	8.0	56.3
S 13	11 30.5	32.7	195 46.5	11.3	14 25.3	8.1	56.3
D 14	26 30.5	31.8	210 16.8	11.4	14 17.2	8.2	56.3
A 15	41 30.6 ··	30.9	224 47.2	11.4	14 09.0	8.3	56.2
Y 16	56 30.7	30.0	239 17.6	11.5	14 00.7	8.3	56.2
17	71 30.7	29.1	253 48.1	11.6	13 52.4	8.3	56.2
18	86 30.8	S11 28.2	268 18.7	11.6	N13 44.1	8.5	56.2
19	101 30.8	27.3	282 49.3	11.7	13 35.6	8.5	56.2
20	116 30.9	26.5	297 20.0	11.7	13 27.1	8.5	56.1
21	131 30.9 ··	25.6	311 50.7	11.9	13 18.6	8.7	56.1
22	146 31.0	24.7	326 21.6	11.8	13 09.9	8.6	56.1
23	161 31.1	23.8	340 52.4	11.9	13 01.3	8.8	56.1
19 00	176 31.1	S11 22.9	355 23.3	12.0	N12 52.5	8.8	56.1
01	191 31.2	22.0	9 54.3	12.1	12 43.7	8.8	56.0
02	206 31.2	21.1	24 25.4	12.1	12 34.9	8.9	56.0
03	221 31.3 ··	20.2	38 56.5	12.2	12 26.0	8.9	56.0
04	236 31.4	19.4	53 27.7	12.2	12 17.1	9.1	56.0
05	251 31.4	18.5	67 58.9	12.3	12 08.0	9.0	55.9
06	266 31.5	S11 17.6	82 30.2	12.3	N11 59.0	9.1	55.9
07	281 31.5	16.7	97 01.5	12.5	11 49.9	9.2	55.9
T 08	296 31.6	15.8	111 33.0	12.4	11 40.7	9.2	55.9
H 09	311 31.7 ··	14.9	126 04.4	12.5	11 31.5	9.2	55.9
U 10	326 31.7	14.0	140 35.9	12.6	11 22.3	9.3	55.8
R 11	341 31.8	13.1	155 07.5	12.7	11 13.0	9.4	55.8
S 12	356 31.8	S11 12.2	169 39.2	12.7	N11 03.6	9.4	55.8
D 13	11 31.9	11.3	184 10.9	12.7	10 54.2	9.4	55.8
A 14	26 32.0	10.4	198 42.6	12.8	10 44.8	9.5	55.8
Y 15	41 32.0 ··	09.6	213 14.4	12.9	10 35.3	9.5	55.7
16	56 32.1	08.7	227 46.3	12.9	10 25.8	9.5	55.7
17	71 32.2	07.8	242 18.2	13.0	10 16.3	9.6	55.7
18	86 32.2	S11 06.9	256 50.2	13.0	N10 06.7	9.7	55.7
19	101 32.3	06.0	271 22.2	13.1	9 57.0	9.7	55.7
20	116 32.4	05.1	285 54.3	13.1	9 47.3	9.7	55.6
21	131 32.4 ··	04.2	300 26.4	13.2	9 37.6	9.7	55.6
22	146 32.5	03.3	314 58.6	13.2	9 27.9	9.8	55.6
23	161 32.5	02.4	329 30.8	13.3	9 18.1	9.8	55.6
20 00	176 32.6	S11 01.5	344 03.1	13.3	N 9 08.3	9.9	55.5
01	191 32.7	11 00.6	358 35.4	13.4	8 58.4	9.9	55.5
02	206 32.7	10 59.7	13 07.8	13.5	8 48.5	9.9	55.5
03	221 32.8 ··	58.8	27 40.3	13.5	8 38.6	10.0	55.5
04	236 32.9	57.9	42 12.8	13.5	8 28.6	9.9	55.5
05	251 32.9	57.0	56 45.3	13.6	8 18.7	10.1	55.4
06	266 33.0	S10 56.1	71 17.9	13.6	N 8 08.6	10.0	55.4
07	281 33.1	55.2	85 50.5	13.7	7 58.6	10.1	55.4
08	296 33.1	54.3	100 23.2	13.7	7 48.5	10.1	55.4
F 09	311 33.2 ··	53.4	114 55.9	13.8	7 38.4	10.1	55.4
R 10	326 33.3	52.5	129 28.7	13.8	7 28.3	10.1	55.3
I 11	341 33.4	51.6	144 01.5	13.9	7 18.2	10.1	55.3
D 12	356 33.4	S10 50.7	158 34.4	13.9	N 7 08.0	10.2	55.3
A 13	11 33.5	49.8	173 07.3	13.9	6 57.8	10.2	55.3
Y 14	26 33.6	48.9	187 40.2	14.0	6 47.6	10.3	55.3
15	41 33.6 ··	48.0	202 13.2	14.1	6 37.3	10.2	55.2
16	56 33.7	47.1	216 46.3	14.1	6 27.1	10.3	55.2
17	71 33.8	46.2	231 19.4	14.1	6 16.8	10.3	55.2
18	86 33.8	S10 45.3	245 52.5	14.1	N 6 06.5	10.4	55.2
19	101 33.9	44.4	260 25.6	14.3	5 56.1	10.3	55.2
20	116 34.0	43.5	274 58.9	14.2	5 45.8	10.4	55.2
21	131 34.1 ··	42.6	289 32.1	14.3	5 35.4	10.3	55.1
22	146 34.1	41.7	304 05.4	14.3	5 25.1	10.4	55.1
23	161 34.2	40.8	318 38.7	14.3	5 14.7	10.4	55.1
	S.D. 16.2	d 0.9	S.D. 15.3		15.2		15.1

Twilight, Sunrise, Moonrise

Lat.	Twilight Naut.	Twilight Civil	Sunrise	Moonrise 18	Moonrise 19	Moonrise 20	Moonrise 21
N 72	05 58	07 16	08 31	14 38	16 35	18 23	20 04
N 70	05 58	07 09	08 15	15 08	16 52	18 31	20 07
68	05 57	07 02	08 02	15 30	17 06	18 39	20 08
66	05 57	06 57	07 51	15 47	17 17	18 44	20 10
64	05 57	06 52	07 42	16 01	17 26	18 49	20 11
62	05 56	06 48	07 34	16 13	17 34	18 54	20 12
60	05 56	06 44	07 27	16 23	17 41	18 58	20 13
N 58	05 55	06 41	07 22	16 31	17 47	19 01	20 14
56	05 55	06 38	07 16	16 39	17 52	19 04	20 14
54	05 54	06 35	07 12	16 45	17 56	19 06	20 15
52	05 54	06 33	07 07	16 51	18 01	19 09	20 16
50	05 53	06 30	07 03	16 57	18 04	19 11	20 16
45	05 51	06 25	06 55	17 09	18 13	19 16	20 17
N 40	05 49	06 20	06 48	17 18	18 20	19 20	20 18
35	05 47	06 16	06 42	17 27	18 26	19 23	20 19
30	05 44	06 12	06 36	17 34	18 31	19 26	20 20
20	05 39	06 05	06 27	17 46	18 40	19 31	20 21
N 10	05 32	05 57	06 19	17 57	18 47	19 36	20 22
0	05 25	05 49	06 11	18 07	18 55	19 40	20 23
S 10	05 16	05 41	06 02	18 18	19 02	19 44	20 24
20	05 04	05 31	05 54	18 28	19 10	19 49	20 26
30	04 49	05 19	05 43	18 41	19 19	19 54	20 27
35	04 40	05 11	05 38	18 48	19 24	19 57	20 28
40	04 28	05 02	05 31	18 56	19 30	20 00	20 29
45	04 14	04 52	05 23	19 05	19 36	20 04	20 30
S 50	03 55	04 39	05 13	19 17	19 44	20 08	20 31
52	03 46	04 32	05 09	19 22	19 48	20 11	20 31
54	03 36	04 25	05 04	19 28	19 52	20 13	20 32
56	03 24	04 17	04 59	19 34	19 56	20 15	20 33
58	03 09	04 08	04 52	19 41	20 01	20 18	20 33
S 60	02 52	03 58	04 46	19 49	20 07	20 21	20 34

Sunset, Twilight, Moonset

Lat.	Sunset	Twilight Civil	Twilight Naut.	Moonset 18	Moonset 19	Moonset 20	Moonset 21
N 72	15 58	17 13	18 33	09 27	09 09	08 56	08 45
N 70	16 14	17 21	18 32	08 56	08 50	08 46	08 41
68	16 27	17 27	18 32	08 33	08 36	08 37	08 37
66	16 38	17 32	18 32	08 15	08 23	08 29	08 34
64	16 47	17 37	18 32	08 00	08 13	08 23	08 31
62	16 55	17 41	18 33	07 47	08 04	08 17	08 28
60	17 01	17 45	18 33	07 37	07 57	08 13	08 26
N 58	17 07	17 48	18 34	07 28	07 50	08 08	08 24
56	17 12	17 51	18 34	07 19	07 44	08 05	08 23
54	17 17	17 53	18 35	07 12	07 39	08 01	08 21
52	17 21	17 56	18 35	07 06	07 34	07 58	08 20
50	17 25	17 58	18 36	07 00	07 30	07 55	08 19
45	17 33	18 03	18 38	06 47	07 20	07 49	08 16
N 40	17 40	18 08	18 40	06 36	07 12	07 44	08 13
35	17 46	18 12	18 42	06 27	07 05	07 40	08 11
30	17 52	18 16	18 44	06 19	06 59	07 36	08 10
20	18 01	18 23	18 49	06 05	06 49	07 29	08 06
N 10	18 09	18 31	18 55	05 53	06 39	07 23	08 04
0	18 17	18 38	19 03	05 42	06 31	07 17	08 01
S 10	18 25	18 47	19 12	05 30	06 22	07 11	07 58
20	18 34	18 56	19 23	05 18	06 12	07 05	07 55
30	18 44	19 09	19 38	05 04	06 01	06 57	07 52
35	18 50	19 16	19 47	04 55	05 55	06 53	07 50
40	18 56	19 25	19 59	04 46	05 48	06 49	07 48
45	19 04	19 35	20 13	04 35	05 39	06 43	07 45
S 50	19 13	19 48	20 31	04 21	05 29	06 36	07 42
52	19 18	19 54	20 40	04 15	05 25	06 33	07 41
54	19 23	20 01	20 50	04 08	05 19	06 30	07 39
56	19 28	20 09	21 02	04 00	05 14	06 26	07 38
58	19 34	20 18	21 16	03 51	05 07	06 22	07 36
S 60	19 40	20 28	21 33	03 41	05 00	06 17	07 34

SUN and MOON

Day	SUN Eqn. of Time 00h	SUN Eqn. of Time 12h	SUN Mer. Pass.	MOON Mer. Pass. Upper	MOON Mer. Pass. Lower	Age	Phase
	m s	m s	h m	h m	h m	d	
18	14 01	13 58	12 14	24 19	11 55	14	
19	13 56	13 53	12 14	00 19	12 43	15	
20	13 50	13 46	12 14	01 06	13 28	16	○

42   FEBRUARY 18, 19, 20 (WED., THURS., FRI.)

G.M.T.	ARIES G.H.A.	VENUS −3.4 G.H.A.	Dec.	MARS +1.4 G.H.A.	Dec.	JUPITER −1.9 G.H.A.	Dec.	SATURN +0.8 G.H.A.	Dec.	STARS Name	S.H.A.	Dec.
18 00	147 52.1	187 53.9 S16	40.2	167 09.0 S 9	12.2	318 34.2 S 2	21.6	318 35.9 S 1	12.0	Acamar	315 37.1	S40 23.2
01	162 54.6	202 53.3	39.3	182 09.6	11.5	333 36.8	21.6	333 38.5	11.9	Achernar	335 45.4	S57 20.3
02	177 57.0	217 52.6	38.4	197 10.2	10.7	348 39.4	21.5	348 41.1	11.9	Acrux	173 36.3	S62 59.5
03	192 59.5	232 51.9 ··	37.5	212 10.9 ··	10.0	3 42.1 ··	21.4	3 43.6 ··	11.8	Adhara	255 31.6	S28 57.0
04	208 02.0	247 51.3	36.6	227 11.5	09.2	18 44.7	21.3	18 46.2	11.8	Aldebaran	291 17.6	N16 28.2
05	223 04.4	262 50.6	35.7	242 12.1	08.4	33 47.3	21.2	33 48.8	11.7			
06	238 06.9	277 50.0 S16	34.9	257 12.7 S 9	07.7	48 49.9 S 2	21.2	48 51.4 S 1	11.6	Alioth	166 41.9	N56 03.6
W 07	253 09.3	292 49.3	34.0	272 13.3	06.9	63 52.6	21.1	63 53.9	11.6	Alkaid	153 18.0	N49 24.3
E 08	268 11.8	307 48.6	33.1	287 13.9	06.2	78 55.2	21.0	78 56.5	11.5	Al Na'ir	28 15.0	S47 03.3
D 09	283 14.3	322 48.0 ··	32.2	302 14.6 ··	05.4	93 57.8 ··	20.9	93 59.1 ··	11.5	Alnilam	276 11.2	S 1 13.0
N 10	298 16.7	337 47.3	31.3	317 15.2	04.7	109 00.5	20.8	109 01.7	11.4	Alphard	218 20.0	S 8 34.7
E 11	313 19.2	352 46.6	30.4	332 15.8	03.9	124 03.1	20.7	124 04.3	11.4			
S 12	328 21.7	7 46.0 S16	29.5	347 16.4 S 9	03.2	139 05.7 S 2	20.7	139 06.8 S 1	11.3	Alphecca	126 31.8	N26 46.5
D 13	343 24.1	22 45.3	28.6	2 17.0	02.4	154 08.4	20.6	154 09.4	11.2	Alpheratz	358 09.3	N28 59.1
A 14	358 26.6	37 44.7	27.7	17 17.7	01.6	169 11.0	20.5	169 12.0	11.2	Altair	62 32.5	N 8 49.0
Y 15	13 29.1	52 44.0 ··	26.8	32 18.3 ··	00.9	184 13.6 ··	20.4	184 14.6 ··	11.1	Ankaa	353 40.3	S42 24.8
16	28 31.5	67 43.4	25.9	47 18.9 9	00.1	199 16.3	20.3	199 17.1	11.1	Antares	112 56.5	S26 23.3
17	43 34.0	82 42.7	25.0	62 19.5 8	59.4	214 18.9	20.2	214 19.7	11.0			
18	58 36.4	97 42.0 S16	24.1	77 20.1 S 8	58.6	229 21.6 S 2	20.2	229 22.3 S 1	10.9	Arcturus	146 18.1	N19 16.7
19	73 38.9	112 41.4	23.2	92 20.8	57.9	244 24.2	20.1	244 24.9	10.9	Atria	108 20.7	S68 59.3
20	88 41.4	127 40.7	22.3	107 21.4	57.1	259 26.8	20.0	259 27.5	10.8	Avior	234 27.5	S59 27.1
21	103 43.8	142 40.1 ··	21.4	122 22.0 ··	56.4	274 29.5 ··	19.9	274 30.0 ··	10.8	Bellatrix	278 58.3	N 6 19.8
22	118 46.3	157 39.4	20.5	137 22.6	55.6	289 32.1	19.8	289 32.6	10.7	Betelgeuse	271 27.8	N 7 24.1
23	133 48.8	172 38.8	19.6	152 23.2	54.8	304 34.7	19.7	304 35.2	10.7			
19 00	148 51.2	187 38.1 S16	18.7	167 23.9 S 8	54.1	319 37.4 S 2	19.7	319 37.8 S 1	10.6	Canopus	264 06.7	S52 41.5
01	163 53.7	202 37.5	17.8	182 24.5	53.3	334 40.0	19.6	334 40.4	10.5	Capella	281 10.7	N45 58.8
02	178 56.2	217 36.8	16.9	197 25.1	52.6	349 42.6	19.5	349 42.9	10.5	Deneb	49 48.7	N45 12.6
03	193 58.6	232 36.2 ··	16.0	212 25.7 ··	51.8	4 45.3 ··	19.4	4 45.5 ··	10.4	Denebola	182 58.5	N14 40.6
04	209 01.1	247 35.5	15.1	227 26.4	51.0	19 47.9	19.3	19 48.1	10.4	Diphda	349 20.8	S18 05.7
05	224 03.6	262 34.9	14.2	242 27.0	50.3	34 50.6	19.2	34 50.7	10.3			
06	239 06.0	277 34.2 S16	13.3	257 27.6 S 8	49.5	49 53.2 S 2	19.2	49 53.2 S 1	10.2	Dubhe	194 21.1	N61 51.1
07	254 08.5	292 33.6	12.3	272 28.2	48.8	64 55.8	19.1	64 55.8	10.2	Elnath	278 43.6	N28 35.5
T 08	269 10.9	307 32.9	11.4	287 28.8	48.0	79 58.5	19.0	79 58.4	10.1	Eltanin	90 57.9	N51 29.2
H 09	284 13.4	322 32.3 ··	10.5	302 29.5 ··	47.3	95 01.1 ··	18.9	95 01.0 ··	10.1	Enif	34 11.6	N 9 47.1
U 10	299 15.9	337 31.6	09.6	317 30.1	46.5	110 03.7	18.8	110 03.6	10.0	Fomalhaut	15 51.4	S29 43.5
R 11	314 18.3	352 31.0	08.7	332 30.7	45.7	125 06.4	18.7	125 06.2	09.9			
S 12	329 20.8	7 30.3 S16	07.8	347 31.3 S 8	45.0	140 09.0 S 2	18.7	140 08.7 S 1	09.9	Gacrux	172 27.9	S57 00.3
D 13	344 23.3	22 29.7	06.9	2 32.0	44.2	155 11.7	18.6	155 11.3	09.8	Gienah	176 17.4	S17 26.2
A 14	359 25.7	37 29.0	06.0	17 32.6	43.5	170 14.3	18.5	170 13.9	09.8	Hadar	149 22.6	S60 16.7
Y 15	14 28.2	52 28.4 ··	05.0	32 33.2 ··	42.7	185 16.9 ··	18.4	185 16.5 ··	09.7	Hamal	328 28.7	N23 22.3
16	29 30.7	67 27.8	04.1	47 33.8	41.9	200 19.6	18.3	200 19.1	09.6	Kaus Aust.	84 16.7	S34 23.6
17	44 33.1	82 27.1	03.2	62 34.5	41.2	215 22.2	18.2	215 21.6	09.6			
18	59 35.6	97 26.5 S16	02.3	77 35.1 S 8	40.4	230 24.9 S 2	18.1	230 24.2 S 1	09.5	Kochab	137 18.7	N74 13.7
19	74 38.1	112 25.8	01.4	92 35.7	39.7	245 27.5	18.1	245 26.8	09.5	Markab	14 03.2	N15 06.1
20	89 40.5	127 25.2 16	00.4	107 36.3	38.9	260 30.2	18.0	260 29.4	09.4	Menkar	314 40.9	N 4 00.8
21	104 43.0	142 24.5 15	59.5	122 36.9 ··	38.1	275 32.8 ··	17.9	275 32.0 ··	09.3	Menkent	148 36.5	S36 16.5
22	119 45.4	157 23.9	58.6	137 37.6	37.4	290 35.4	17.8	290 34.5	09.3	Miaplacidus	221 43.9	S69 38.5
23	134 47.9	172 23.3	57.7	152 38.2	36.6	305 38.1	17.7	305 37.1	09.2			
20 00	149 50.4	187 22.6 S15	56.8	167 38.8 S 8	35.9	320 40.7 S 2	17.6	320 39.7 S 1	09.2	Mirfak	309 15.7	N49 47.8
01	164 52.8	202 22.0	55.8	182 39.4	35.1	335 43.4	17.5	335 42.3	09.1	Nunki	76 29.1	S26 19.2
02	179 55.3	217 21.3	54.9	197 40.1	34.3	350 46.0	17.5	350 44.9	09.0	Peacock	53 58.5	S56 47.7
03	194 57.8	232 20.7 ··	54.0	212 40.7 ··	33.6	5 48.7 ··	17.4	5 47.5 ··	09.0	Pollux	243 57.5	N28 04.3
04	210 00.2	247 20.1	53.1	227 41.3	32.8	20 51.3	17.3	20 50.0	08.9	Procyon	245 25.2	N 5 16.3
05	225 02.7	262 19.4	52.1	242 41.9	32.1	35 53.9	17.2	35 52.6	08.9			
06	240 05.2	277 18.8 S15	51.2	257 42.6 S 8	31.3	50 56.6 S 2	17.1	50 55.2 S 1	08.8	Rasalhague	96 29.5	N12 34.3
07	255 07.6	292 18.1	50.3	272 43.2	30.5	65 59.2	17.0	65 57.8	08.7	Regulus	208 09.4	N12 03.5
08	270 10.1	307 17.5	49.3	287 43.8	29.8	81 01.9	16.9	81 00.4	08.7	Rigel	281 35.6	S 8 13.6
F 09	285 12.5	322 16.9 ··	48.4	302 44.5 ··	29.0	96 04.5 ··	16.9	96 03.0 ··	08.6	Rigil Kent.	140 25.2	S60 45.1
R 10	300 15.0	337 16.2	47.5	317 45.1	28.3	111 07.2	16.8	111 05.5	08.6	Sabik	102 40.9	S15 42.1
I 11	315 17.5	352 15.6	46.6	332 45.7	27.5	126 09.8	16.7	126 08.1	08.5			
D 12	330 19.9	7 15.0 S15	45.6	347 46.3 S 8	26.7	141 12.5 S 2	16.6	141 10.7 S 1	08.4	Schedar	350 09.1	N56 26.1
A 13	345 22.4	22 14.3	44.7	2 47.0	26.0	156 15.1	16.5	156 13.3	08.4	Shaula	96 55.5	S37 05.3
Y 14	0 24.9	37 13.7	43.8	17 47.6	25.2	171 17.7	16.4	171 15.9	08.3	Sirius	258 55.2	S16 41.7
15	15 27.3	52 13.1 ··	42.8	32 48.2 ··	24.4	186 20.4 ··	16.3	186 18.5 ··	08.3	Spica	158 57.0	S11 03.8
16	30 29.8	67 12.4	41.9	47 48.8	23.7	201 23.0	16.2	201 21.1	08.2	Suhail	223 10.1	S43 21.5
17	45 32.3	82 11.8	41.0	62 49.5	22.9	216 25.7	16.2	216 23.6	08.1			
18	60 34.7	97 11.2 S15	40.0	77 50.1 S 8	22.2	231 28.3 S 2	16.1	231 26.2 S 1	08.1	Vega	80 55.9	N38 45.8
19	75 37.2	112 10.5	39.1	92 50.7	21.4	246 31.0	16.0	246 28.8	08.0	Zuben'ubi	137 32.6	S15 57.8
20	90 39.7	127 09.9	38.1	107 51.3	20.6	261 33.6	15.9	261 31.4	07.9		S.H.A.	Mer. Pass.
21	105 42.1	142 09.3 ··	37.2	122 52.0 ··	19.9	276 36.3 ··	15.8	276 34.0 ··	07.9	Venus	38 46.9	11 30
22	120 44.6	157 08.7	36.3	137 52.6	19.1	291 38.9	15.7	291 36.6	07.8	Mars	18 32.6	12 50
23	135 47.0	172 08.0	35.3	152 53.2	18.3	306 41.6	15.6	306 39.1	07.8	Jupiter	170 46.1	2 41
Mer. Pass.	14 02.3	v 0.6	d 0.9	v 0.6	d 0.8	v 2.6	d 0.1	v 2.6	d 0.1	Saturn	170 46.5	2 41

AUGUST 2, 3, 4 (SUN., MON., TUES.)   153

SUN and MOON

G.M.T.	SUN GHA	Dec.	MOON GHA	v	Dec.	d	H.P.
2 00	178 26.7	N17 50.7	154 42.5	10.8	N13 00.9	9.7	57.3
01	193 26.8	50.1	169 12.3	10.9	12 51.2	9.7	57.3
02	208 26.8	49.4	183 42.2	11.0	12 41.5	9.7	57.2
03	223 26.8 ..	48.8	198 12.2	11.0	12 31.8	9.8	57.2
04	238 26.9	48.1	212 42.2	11.1	12 22.0	9.9	57.2
05	253 26.9	47.5	227 12.3	11.2	12 12.1	9.9	57.1
06	268 27.0	N17 46.9	241 42.5	11.3	N12 02.2	9.9	57.1
07	283 27.0	46.2	256 12.8	11.3	11 52.3	10.1	57.1
08	298 27.0	45.6	270 43.1	11.4	11 42.2	10.0	57.0
S 09	313 27.1 ..	44.9	285 13.5	11.5	11 32.2	10.1	57.0
U 10	328 27.1	44.3	299 44.0	11.6	11 22.1	10.2	57.0
N 11	343 27.2	43.7	314 14.6	11.6	11 11.9	10.2	57.0
D 12	358 27.2	N17 43.0	328 45.2	11.7	N11 01.7	10.2	56.9
A 13	13 27.3	42.4	343 15.9	11.8	10 51.5	10.3	56.9
Y 14	28 27.3	41.7	357 46.7	11.9	10 41.2	10.3	56.9
15	43 27.4 ..	41.1	12 17.6	11.9	10 30.9	10.4	56.8
16	58 27.4	40.4	26 48.5	12.0	10 20.5	10.4	56.8
17	73 27.5	39.8	41 19.5	12.1	10 10.1	10.4	56.8
18	88 27.5	N17 39.1	55 50.6	12.1	N 9 59.7	10.5	56.7
19	103 27.5	38.5	70 21.7	12.2	9 49.2	10.5	56.7
20	118 27.6	37.9	84 52.9	12.3	9 38.7	10.5	56.7
21	133 27.6 ..	37.2	99 24.2	12.3	9 28.2	10.6	56.7
22	148 27.7	36.6	113 55.5	12.4	9 17.6	10.6	56.6
23	163 27.7	35.9	128 26.9	12.5	9 07.0	10.7	56.6
3 00	178 27.8	N17 35.3	142 58.4	12.6	N 8 56.3	10.7	56.6
01	193 27.8	34.6	157 30.0	12.6	8 45.6	10.7	56.5
02	208 27.9	34.0	172 01.6	12.6	8 34.9	10.7	56.5
03	223 27.9 ..	33.3	186 33.2	12.8	8 24.2	10.8	56.5
04	238 28.0	32.7	201 05.0	12.8	8 13.4	10.8	56.4
05	253 28.0	32.0	215 36.8	12.8	8 02.6	10.8	56.4
06	268 28.1	N17 31.4	230 08.6	12.9	N 7 51.8	10.8	56.4
07	283 28.1	30.7	244 40.5	13.0	7 41.0	10.9	56.4
08	298 28.2	30.0	259 12.5	13.0	7 30.1	10.9	56.3
M 09	313 28.2 ..	29.4	273 44.5	13.1	7 19.2	10.9	56.3
O 10	328 28.3	28.7	288 16.6	13.2	7 08.3	10.9	56.3
N 11	343 28.3	28.1	302 48.8	13.2	6 57.4	11.0	56.2
D 12	358 28.4	N17 27.4	317 21.0	13.3	N 6 46.4	10.9	56.2
A 13	13 28.4	26.8	331 53.3	13.3	6 35.5	11.0	56.2
Y 14	28 28.5	26.1	346 25.6	13.4	6 24.5	11.0	56.2
15	43 28.5 ..	25.5	0 58.0	13.4	6 13.5	11.0	56.1
16	58 28.6	24.8	15 30.4	13.5	6 02.5	11.1	56.1
17	73 28.6	24.1	30 02.9	13.5	5 51.4	11.0	56.1
18	88 28.7	N17 23.5	44 35.4	13.6	N 5 40.4	11.1	56.0
19	103 28.7	22.8	59 08.0	13.7	5 29.3	11.1	56.0
20	118 28.8	22.2	73 40.7	13.7	5 18.2	11.0	56.0
21	133 28.8 ..	21.5	88 13.4	13.7	5 07.2	11.1	56.0
22	148 28.9	20.9	102 46.1	13.8	4 56.1	11.1	55.9
23	163 28.9	20.2	117 18.9	13.8	4 45.0	11.2	55.9
4 00	178 29.0	N17 19.5	131 51.7	13.9	N 4 33.8	11.1	55.9
01	193 29.1	18.9	146 24.6	13.9	4 22.7	11.1	55.8
02	208 29.1	18.2	160 57.5	14.0	4 11.6	11.2	55.8
03	223 29.2 ..	17.5	175 30.5	14.0	4 00.4	11.1	55.8
04	238 29.2	16.9	190 03.5	14.1	3 49.3	11.2	55.8
05	253 29.3	16.2	204 36.6	14.1	3 38.1	11.1	55.7
06	268 29.3	N17 15.6	219 09.7	14.2	N 3 27.0	11.2	55.7
07	283 29.4	14.9	233 42.9	14.1	3 15.8	11.1	55.7
08	298 29.4	14.2	248 16.0	14.3	3 04.7	11.2	55.7
T 09	313 29.5 ..	13.6	262 49.3	14.2	2 53.5	11.2	55.6
U 10	328 29.6	12.9	277 22.5	14.3	2 42.3	11.1	55.6
E 11	343 29.6	12.2	291 55.8	14.4	2 31.2	11.2	55.6
S 12	358 29.7	N17 11.6	306 29.2	14.4	N 2 20.0	11.2	55.5
D 13	13 29.7	10.9	321 02.6	14.4	2 08.8	11.1	55.5
A 14	28 29.8	10.2	335 36.0	14.4	1 57.7	11.2	55.5
Y 15	43 29.8 ..	09.6	350 09.4	14.5	1 46.5	11.1	55.5
16	58 29.9	08.9	4 42.9	14.5	1 35.4	11.2	55.4
17	73 30.0	08.2	19 16.4	14.6	1 24.2	11.1	55.4
18	88 30.0	N17 07.5	33 50.0	14.6	N 1 13.1	11.2	55.4
19	103 30.1	06.9	48 23.6	14.6	1 01.9	11.1	55.4
20	118 30.1	06.2	62 57.2	14.6	0 50.8	11.2	55.4
21	133 30.2 ..	05.5	77 30.8	14.7	0 39.6	11.1	55.3
22	148 30.2	04.9	92 04.5	14.7	0 28.5	11.2	55.3
23	163 30.3	04.2	106 38.2	14.7	0 17.4	11.1	55.3
	S.D. 15.8	d 0.7	S.D. 15.5		15.3		15.1

Twilight, Sunrise, Moonrise

Lat.	Naut.	Civil	Sunrise	2	3	4	5
N 72	[ ]	[ ]	[ ]	05 07	07 05	08 54	10 38
N 70	////	////	01 42	05 29	07 17	08 58	10 35
68	////	////	02 24	05 46	07 26	09 01	10 33
66	////	00 51	02 52	06 00	07 34	09 04	10 31
64	////	01 50	03 14	06 11	07 41	09 06	10 29
62	////	02 22	03 31	06 21	07 46	09 08	10 28
60	00 46	02 46	03 45	06 29	07 51	09 10	10 27
N 58	01 39	03 04	03 57	06 36	07 55	09 12	10 26
56	02 09	03 19	04 07	06 43	07 59	09 13	10 25
54	02 31	03 32	04 16	06 48	08 02	09 14	10 24
52	02 49	03 44	04 24	06 53	08 05	09 15	10 23
50	03 03	03 53	04 32	06 58	08 08	09 16	10 23
45	03 32	04 14	04 47	07 08	08 14	09 19	10 21
N 40	03 53	04 30	05 00	07 16	08 19	09 20	10 20
35	04 09	04 43	05 11	07 23	08 24	09 22	10 19
30	04 23	04 54	05 20	07 29	08 27	09 23	10 18
20	04 45	05 13	05 36	07 40	08 34	09 26	10 16
N 10	05 02	05 28	05 50	07 49	08 40	09 28	10 15
0	05 16	05 41	06 03	07 58	08 45	09 30	10 13
S 10	05 28	05 53	06 15	08 06	08 50	09 32	10 12
20	05 39	06 06	06 29	08 15	08 56	09 34	10 11
30	05 50	06 19	06 44	08 26	09 03	09 37	10 09
35	05 56	06 26	06 53	08 32	09 06	09 38	10 08
40	06 02	06 34	07 03	08 39	09 11	09 40	10 07
45	06 08	06 43	07 14	08 47	09 16	09 42	10 06
S 50	06 15	06 54	07 29	08 56	09 21	09 44	10 05
52	06 18	06 58	07 35	09 01	09 24	09 45	10 04
54	06 21	07 04	07 42	09 05	09 27	09 46	10 04
56	06 24	07 09	07 51	09 11	09 30	09 47	10 03
58	06 28	07 15	08 00	09 17	09 34	09 49	10 02
S 60	06 32	07 23	08 10	09 23	09 38	09 50	10 01

Sunset, Twilight, Moonset

Lat.	Sunset	Civil	Naut.	2	3	4	5
N 72	[ ]	[ ]	[ ]	22 23	22 09	21 56	21 44
N 70	22 24	////	////	22 10	22 02	21 56	21 49
68	21 44	////	////	21 58	21 57	21 55	21 53
66	21 17	23 10	////	21 49	21 53	21 55	21 57
64	20 56	22 18	////	21 41	21 49	21 55	22 00
62	20 39	21 47	////	21 35	21 45	21 54	22 03
60	20 26	21 24	23 16	21 29	21 42	21 54	22 05
N 58	20 14	21 06	22 29	21 24	21 40	21 54	22 08
56	20 04	20 51	22 00	21 19	21 37	21 54	22 10
54	19 55	20 38	21 39	21 15	21 35	21 54	22 11
52	19 47	20 27	21 22	21 11	21 33	21 53	22 13
50	19 40	20 18	21 07	21 08	21 31	21 53	22 14
45	19 24	19 58	20 40	21 00	21 28	21 53	22 17
N 40	19 12	19 42	20 19	20 54	21 24	21 53	22 20
35	19 01	19 29	20 02	20 48	21 21	21 52	22 22
30	18 52	19 18	19 49	20 44	21 19	21 52	22 24
20	18 36	18 59	19 27	20 35	21 14	21 52	22 28
N 10	18 22	18 44	19 10	20 28	21 11	21 51	22 31
0	18 10	18 31	18 56	20 21	21 07	21 51	22 34
S 10	17 57	18 19	18 44	20 14	21 03	21 51	22 37
20	17 44	18 07	18 33	20 06	20 59	21 50	22 40
30	17 28	17 54	18 22	19 57	20 55	21 50	22 44
35	17 20	17 46	18 17	19 52	20 52	21 49	22 46
40	17 10	17 39	18 11	19 46	20 49	21 49	22 48
45	16 58	17 30	18 05	19 40	20 45	21 49	22 51
S 50	16 44	17 19	17 58	19 32	20 41	21 48	22 54
52	16 38	17 15	17 55	19 28	20 39	21 48	22 55
54	16 30	17 09	17 52	19 24	20 37	21 48	22 57
56	16 22	17 04	17 49	19 19	20 35	21 48	22 59
58	16 13	16 57	17 45	19 14	20 32	21 47	23 01
S 60	16 03	16 51	17 42	19 08	20 29	21 47	23 03

SUN and MOON

Day	SUN Eqn. of Time 00ʰ	12ʰ	Mer. Pass.	MOON Mer. Pass. Upper	Lower	Age	Phase
2	06 13	06 11	12 06	14 09	01 45	02	
3	06 09	06 07	12 06	14 56	02 33	03	
4	06 04	06 01	12 06	15 41	03 19	04	

154   **AUGUST 5, 6, 7 (WED., THURS., FRI.)**

G.M.T.	ARIES G.H.A.	VENUS −3.4 G.H.A.	Dec.	MARS +1.8 G.H.A.	Dec.	JUPITER −1.4 G.H.A.	Dec.	SATURN +1.2 G.H.A.	Dec.	STARS Name	S.H.A.	Dec.
5 00	313 27.4	147 55.5 N 7	35.1	210 34.7 N23	35.0	126 46.9 S 1	35.7	127 07.7 S 0	14.6	Acamar	315 36.8	S40 22.5
01	328 29.8	162 55.2	33.9	225 35.4	34.8	141 49.0	35.8	142 10.0	14.7	Achernar	335 44.6	S57 19.6
02	343 32.3	177 54.9	32.7	240 36.1	34.7	156 51.1	36.0	157 12.2	14.8	Acrux	173 37.0	S62 59.9
03	358 34.8	192 54.6 ··	31.5	255 36.7 ··	34.6	171 53.2 ··	36.2	172 14.5 ··	14.9	Adhara	255 32.0	S28 56.7
04	13 37.2	207 54.3	30.2	270 37.4	34.5	186 55.3	36.3	187 16.8	15.0	Aldebaran	291 17.4	N16 28.3
05	28 39.7	222 54.0	29.0	285 38.1	34.3	201 57.4	36.5	202 19.0	15.1			
06	43 42.2	237 53.7 N 7	27.8	300 38.7 N23	34.2	216 59.4 S 1	36.7	217 21.3 S 0	15.2	Alioth	166 42.2	N56 04.0
07	58 44.6	252 53.4	26.6	315 39.4	34.1	232 01.5	36.9	232 23.6	15.3	Alkaid	153 18.1	N49 24.7
08	73 47.1	267 53.1	25.3	330 40.1	34.0	247 03.6	37.0	247 25.8	15.4	Al Na'ir	28 13.7	S47 02.9
09	88 49.6	282 52.8 ··	24.1	345 40.7 ··	33.9	262 05.7 ··	37.2	262 28.1 ··	15.5	Alnilam	276 11.3	S 1 12.8
10	103 52.0	297 52.5	22.9	0 41.4	33.7	277 07.8	37.4	277 30.3	15.5	Alphard	218 20.3	S 8 34.6
11	118 54.5	312 52.2	21.7	15 42.1	33.6	292 09.9	37.5	292 32.6	15.6			
12	133 57.0	327 51.9 N 7	20.4	30 42.7 N23	33.5	307 12.0 S 1	37.7	307 34.9 S 0	15.7	Alphecca	126 31.5	N26 46.9
13	148 59.4	342 51.6	19.2	45 43.4	33.4	322 14.1	37.9	322 37.1	15.8	Alpheratz	358 08.4	N28 59.2
14	164 01.9	357 51.3	18.0	60 44.1	33.2	337 16.2	38.0	337 39.4	15.9	Altair	62 31.6	N 8 49.3
15	179 04.3	12 51.0 ··	16.7	75 44.7 ··	33.1	352 18.2 ··	38.2	352 41.7 ··	16.0	Ankaa	353 39.4	S42 24.2
16	194 06.8	27 50.7	15.5	90 45.4	33.0	7 20.3	38.4	7 43.9	16.1	Antares	112 55.9	S26 23.5
17	209 09.3	42 50.4	14.3	105 46.1	32.9	22 22.4	38.5	22 46.2	16.2			
18	224 11.7	57 50.1 N 7	13.1	120 46.7 N23	32.7	37 24.5 S 1	38.7	37 48.4 S 0	16.3	Arcturus	146 18.0	N19 17.0
19	239 14.2	72 49.8	11.8	135 47.4	32.6	52 26.6	38.9	52 50.7	16.4	Atria	108 19.3	S68 59.9
20	254 16.7	87 49.5	10.6	150 48.1	32.5	67 28.7	39.0	67 53.0	16.5	Avior	234 28.6	S59 26.9
21	269 19.1	102 49.2 ··	09.4	165 48.8 ··	32.4	82 30.8 ··	39.2	82 55.2 ··	16.6	Bellatrix	278 58.3	N 6 20.0
22	284 21.6	117 48.9	08.1	180 49.4	32.2	97 32.9	39.4	97 57.5	16.7	Betelgeuse	271 27.9	N 7 24.3
23	299 24.1	132 48.6	06.9	195 50.1	32.1	112 34.9	39.6	112 59.7	16.8			
6 00	314 26.5	147 48.3 N 7	05.7	210 50.8 N23	32.0	127 37.0 S 1	39.7	128 02.0 S 0	16.9	Canopus	264 07.4	S52 41.0
01	329 29.0	162 48.0	04.4	225 51.4	31.8	142 39.1	39.9	143 04.3	17.0	Capella	281 10.7	N45 58.6
02	344 31.5	177 47.7	03.2	240 52.1	31.7	157 41.2	40.1	158 06.5	17.1	Deneb	49 47.6	N45 12.9
03	359 33.9	192 47.4 ··	02.0	255 52.8 ··	31.6	172 43.3 ··	40.2	173 08.8 ··	17.2	Denebola	182 58.7	N14 40.7
04	14 36.4	207 47.2 7	00.7	270 53.4	31.5	187 45.4	40.4	188 11.0	17.3	Diphda	349 20.1	S18 05.2
05	29 38.8	222 46.9 6	59.5	285 54.1	31.3	202 47.5	40.6	203 13.3	17.3			
06	44 41.3	237 46.6 N 6	58.3	300 54.8 N23	31.2	217 49.5 S 1	40.7	218 15.6 S 0	17.4	Dubhe	194 21.9	N61 51.3
07	59 43.8	252 46.3	57.0	315 55.5	31.1	232 51.6	40.9	233 17.8	17.5	Elnath	278 43.6	N28 35.5
08	74 46.2	267 46.0	55.8	330 56.1	30.9	247 53.7	41.1	248 20.1	17.6	Eltanin	90 57.1	N51 29.8
09	89 48.7	282 45.7 ··	54.6	345 56.8 ··	30.8	262 55.8 ··	41.3	263 22.3 ··	17.7	Enif	34 10.7	N 9 47.5
10	104 51.2	297 45.4	53.3	0 57.5	30.7	277 57.9	41.4	278 24.6	17.8	Fomalhaut	15 50.4	S29 43.1
11	119 53.6	312 45.1	52.1	15 58.1	30.5	293 00.0	41.6	293 26.9	17.9			
12	134 56.1	327 44.8 N 6	50.9	30 58.8 N23	30.4	308 02.1 S 1	41.8	308 29.1 S 0	18.0	Gacrux	172 28.4	S57 00.7
13	149 58.6	342 44.5	49.6	45 59.5	30.3	323 04.1	41.9	323 31.4	18.1	Gienah	176 17.5	S17 26.3
14	165 01.0	357 44.2	48.4	61 00.2	30.1	338 06.2	42.1	338 33.6	18.2	Hadar	149 22.6	S60 17.2
15	180 03.5	12 43.9 ··	47.1	76 00.8 ··	30.0	353 08.3 ··	42.3	353 35.9 ··	18.3	Hamal	328 28.2	N23 22.4
16	195 06.0	27 43.6	45.9	91 01.5	29.9	8 10.4	42.4	8 38.2	18.4	Kaus Aust.	84 15.7	S34 23.6
17	210 08.4	42 43.4	44.7	106 02.2	29.7	23 12.5	42.6	23 40.4	18.5			
18	225 10.9	57 43.1 N 6	43.4	121 02.8 N23	29.6	38 14.6 S 1	42.8	38 42.7 S 0	18.6	Kochab	137 19.0	N74 14.3
19	240 13.3	72 42.8	42.2	136 03.5	29.5	53 16.6	43.0	53 44.9	18.7	Markab	14 02.3	N15 06.3
20	255 15.8	87 42.5	41.0	151 04.2	29.3	68 18.7	43.1	68 47.2	18.8	Menkar	314 40.5	N 4 01.0
21	270 18.3	102 42.2 ··	39.7	166 04.9 ··	29.2	83 20.8 ··	43.3	83 49.4 ··	18.9	Menkent	148 36.4	S36 16.8
22	285 20.7	117 41.9	38.5	181 05.5	29.1	98 22.9	43.5	98 51.7	19.0	Miaplacidus	221 45.7	S69 38.5
23	300 23.2	132 41.6	37.2	196 06.2	28.9	113 25.0	43.6	113 54.0	19.1			
7 00	315 25.7	147 41.3 N 6	36.0	211 06.9 N23	28.8	128 27.1 S 1	43.8	128 56.2 S 0	19.2	Mirfak	309 15.3	N49 47.5
01	330 28.1	162 41.0	34.8	226 07.6	28.7	143 29.1	44.0	143 58.5	19.3	Nunki	76 28.1	S26 19.2
02	345 30.6	177 40.8	33.5	241 08.2	28.5	158 31.2	44.1	159 00.7	19.3	Peacock	53 56.8	S56 47.7
03	0 33.1	192 40.5 ··	32.3	256 08.9 ··	28.4	173 33.3 ··	44.3	174 03.0 ··	19.4	Pollux	243 57.8	N28 04.3
04	15 35.5	207 40.2	31.0	271 09.6	28.3	188 35.4	44.5	189 05.2	19.5	Procyon	245 25.5	N 5 16.4
05	30 38.0	222 39.9	29.8	286 10.3	28.1	203 37.5	44.7	204 07.5	19.6			
06	45 40.4	237 39.6 N 6	28.6	301 10.9 N23	28.0	218 39.6 S 1	44.8	219 09.8 S 0	19.7	Rasalhague	96 28.8	N12 34.6
07	60 42.9	252 39.3	27.3	316 11.6	27.8	233 41.6	45.0	234 12.0	19.8	Regulus	208 09.7	N12 03.6
08	75 45.4	267 39.0	26.1	331 12.3	27.7	248 43.7	45.2	249 14.3	19.9	Rigel	281 35.6	S 8 13.3
09	90 47.8	282 38.8 ··	24.8	346 13.0 ··	27.6	263 45.8 ··	45.3	264 16.5 ··	20.0	Rigil Kent.	140 25.0	S60 45.7
10	105 50.3	297 38.5	23.6	1 13.6	27.4	278 47.9	45.5	279 18.8	20.1	Sabik	102 40.2	S15 42.1
11	120 52.8	312 38.2	22.4	16 14.3	27.3	293 50.0	45.7	294 21.0	20.2			
12	135 55.2	327 37.9 N 6	21.1	31 15.0 N23	27.1	308 52.0 S 1	45.9	309 23.3 S 0	20.3	Schedar	350 08.0	N56 25.9
13	150 57.7	342 37.6	19.9	46 15.7	27.0	323 54.1	46.0	324 25.6	20.4	Shaula	96 54.7	S37 05.5
14	166 00.2	357 37.3	18.6	61 16.3	26.9	338 56.2	46.2	339 27.8	20.5	Sirius	258 55.5	S16 41.4
15	181 02.6	12 37.1 ··	17.4	76 17.0 ··	26.7	353 58.3 ··	46.4	354 30.1 ··	20.6	Spica	158 57.0	S11 03.8
16	196 05.1	27 36.8	16.1	91 17.7	26.6	9 00.4	46.5	9 32.3	20.7	Suhail	223 10.8	S43 21.4
17	211 07.6	42 36.5	14.9	106 18.4	26.4	24 02.4	46.7	24 34.6	20.8			
18	226 10.0	57 36.2 N 6	13.7	121 19.0 N23	26.3	39 04.5 S 1	46.9	39 36.8 S 0	20.9	Vega	80 55.1	N38 46.2
19	241 12.5	72 35.9	12.4	136 19.7	26.2	54 06.6	47.1	54 39.1	21.0	Zuben'ubi	137 32.4	S15 57.8
20	256 14.9	87 35.6	11.2	151 20.4	26.0	69 08.7	47.2	69 41.4	21.1		S.H.A.	Mer. Pass.
21	271 17.4	102 35.4 ··	09.9	166 21.1 ··	25.9	84 10.8 ··	47.4	84 43.6 ··	21.2	Venus	193 21.8	14 09
22	286 19.9	117 35.1	08.7	181 21.7	25.7	99 12.9	47.6	99 45.9	21.3	Mars	256 24.2	9 56
23	301 22.3	132 34.8	07.4	196 22.4	25.6	114 14.9	47.7	114 48.1	21.4	Jupiter	173 10.5	15 27
Mer. Pass.	3 01.7	v −0.3 d 1.2		v 0.7 d 0.1		v 2.1 d 0.2		v 2.3 d 0.1		Saturn	173 35.5	15 26

42ᵐ　INCREMENTS AND CORRECTIONS　43ᵐ

42ᵐ	Sun Planets	Aries	Moon	v or Corrⁿ d	v or Corrⁿ d	v or Corrⁿ d
00	10° 30'.0	10° 31'.8	10° 01'.3	0.0 0.0	6.0 4.3	12.0 8.5
01	10° 30'.3	10° 32'.0	10° 01'.5	0.1 0.1	6.1 4.3	12.1 8.6
02	10° 30'.5	10° 32'.3	10° 01'.8	0.2 0.1	6.2 4.4	12.2 8.6
03	10° 30'.8	10° 32'.5	10° 02'.0	0.3 0.2	6.3 4.5	12.3 8.7
04	10° 31'.0	10° 32'.8	10° 02'.3	0.4 0.3	6.4 4.5	12.4 8.8
05	10° 31'.2	10° 33'.0	10° 02'.5	0.5 0.4	6.5 4.6	12.5 8.9
06	10° 31'.5	10° 33'.3	10° 02'.7	0.6 0.4	6.6 4.7	12.6 8.9
07	10° 31'.8	10° 33'.5	10° 03'.0	0.7 0.5	6.7 4.7	12.7 9.0
08	10° 32'.0	10° 33'.8	10° 03'.2	0.8 0.6	6.8 4.8	12.8 9.1
09	10° 32'.2	10° 34'.0	10° 03'.4	0.9 0.6	6.9 4.9	12.9 9.1
10	10° 32'.5	10° 34'.3	10° 03'.7	1.0 0.7	7.0 5.0	13.0 9.2
11	10° 32'.8	10° 34'.5	10° 03'.9	1.1 0.8	7.1 5.0	13.1 9.3
12	10° 33'.0	10° 34'.8	10° 04'.2	1.2 0.9	7.2 5.1	13.2 9.3
13	10° 33'.2	10° 35'.0	10° 04'.4	1.3 0.9	7.3 5.2	13.3 9.4
14	10° 33'.5	10° 35'.3	10° 04'.6	1.4 1.0	7.4 5.2	13.4 9.5
15	10° 33'.7	10° 35'.5	10° 04'.9	1.5 1.1	7.5 5.3	13.5 9.6
16	10° 34'.0	10° 35'.8	10° 05'.1	1.6 1.1	7.6 5.4	13.6 9.6
17	10° 34'.3	10° 36'.0	10° 05'.4	1.7 1.2	7.7 5.5	13.7 9.7
18	10° 34'.5	10° 36'.3	10° 05'.6	1.8 1.3	7.8 5.5	13.8 9.8
19	10° 34'.7	10° 36'.5	10° 05'.8	1.9 1.3	7.9 5.6	13.9 9.8
20	10° 35'.0	10° 36'.8	10° 06'.1	2.0 1.4	8.0 5.7	14.0 9.9
21	10° 35'.3	10° 37'.0	10° 06'.3	2.1 1.5	8.1 5.7	14.1 10.0
22	10° 35'.5	10° 37'.3	10° 06'.5	2.2 1.6	8.2 5.8	14.2 10.1
23	10° 35'.7	10° 37'.5	10° 06'.8	2.3 1.6	8.3 5.9	14.3 10.1
24	10° 36'.0	10° 37'.8	10° 07'.0	2.4 1.7	8.4 6.0	14.4 10.2
25	10° 36'.2	10° 38'.0	10° 07'.3	2.5 1.8	8.5 6.0	14.5 10.3
26	10° 36'.5	10° 38'.3	10° 07'.5	2.6 1.8	8.6 6.1	14.6 10.3
27	10° 36'.8	10° 38'.5	10° 07'.7	2.7 1.9	8.7 6.2	14.7 10.4
28	10° 37'.0	10° 38'.8	10° 08'.0	2.8 2.0	8.8 6.2	14.8 10.5
29	10° 37'.2	10° 39'.0	10° 08'.2	2.9 2.1	8.9 6.3	14.9 10.6
30	10° 37'.5	10° 39'.3	10° 08'.5	3.0 2.1	9.0 6.4	15.0 10.6
31	10° 37'.8	10° 39'.5	10° 08'.7	3.1 2.2	9.1 6.4	15.1 10.7
32	10° 38'.0	10° 39'.8	10° 08'.9	3.2 2.3	9.2 6.5	15.2 10.8
33	10° 38'.2	10° 40'.0	10° 09'.2	3.3 2.3	9.3 6.6	15.3 10.8
34	10° 38'.5	10° 40'.3	10° 09'.4	3.4 2.4	9.4 6.7	15.4 10.9
35	10° 38'.8	10° 40'.5	10° 09'.7	3.5 2.5	9.5 6.7	15.5 11.0
36	10° 39'.0	10° 40'.8	10° 09'.9	3.6 2.6	9.6 6.8	15.6 11.1
37	10° 39'.3	10° 41'.0	10° 10'.1	3.7 2.6	9.7 6.9	15.7 11.1
38	10° 39'.5	10° 41'.3	10° 10'.4	3.8 2.7	9.8 6.9	15.8 11.2
39	10° 39'.7	10° 41'.5	10° 10'.6	3.9 2.8	9.9 7.0	15.9 11.3
40	10° 40'.0	10° 41'.8	10° 10'.8	4.0 2.8	10.0 7.1	16.0 11.3
41	10° 40'.3	10° 42'.0	10° 11'.1	4.1 2.9	10.1 7.2	16.1 11.4
42	10° 40'.5	10° 42'.3	10° 11'.3	4.2 3.0	10.2 7.2	16.2 11.5
43	10° 40'.7	10° 42'.5	10° 11'.6	4.3 3.0	10.3 7.3	16.3 11.5
44	10° 41'.0	10° 42'.8	10° 11'.8	4.4 3.1	10.4 7.4	16.4 11.6
45	10° 41'.3	10° 43'.0	10° 12'.0	4.5 3.2	10.5 7.4	16.5 11.7
46	10° 41'.5	10° 43'.3	10° 12'.3	4.6 3.3	10.6 7.5	16.6 11.8
47	10° 41'.7	10° 43'.5	10° 12'.5	4.7 3.3	10.7 7.6	16.7 12.1
48	10° 42'.0	10° 43'.8	10° 12'.8	4.8 3.4	10.8 7.7	16.8 11.9
49	10° 42'.2	10° 44'.0	10° 13'.0	4.9 3.5	10.9 7.7	16.9 12.0
50	10° 42'.5	10° 44'.3	10° 13'.2	5.0 3.5	11.0 7.8	17.0 12.0
51	10° 42'.8	10° 44'.5	10° 13'.5	5.1 3.6	11.1 7.9	17.1 12.1
52	10° 43'.0	10° 44'.8	10° 13'.7	5.2 3.7	11.2 7.9	17.2 12.2
53	10° 43'.2	10° 45'.0	10° 13'.9	5.3 3.8	11.3 8.0	17.3 12.3
54	10° 43'.5	10° 45'.3	10° 14'.2	5.4 3.8	11.4 8.1	17.4 12.3
55	10° 43'.8	10° 45'.5	10° 14'.4	5.5 3.9	11.5 8.1	17.5 12.4
56	10° 44'.0	10° 45'.8	10° 14'.7	5.6 4.0	11.6 8.2	17.6 12.5
57	10° 44'.2	10° 46'.0	10° 14'.9	5.7 4.0	11.7 8.3	17.7 12.5
58	10° 44'.5	10° 46'.3	10° 15'.1	5.8 4.1	11.8 8.4	17.8 12.6
59	10° 44'.7	10° 46'.5	10° 15'.4	5.9 4.2	11.9 8.4	17.9 12.7
60	10° 45'.0	10° 46'.8	10° 15'.6	6.0 4.3	12.0 8.5	18.0 12.8

43ᵐ	Sun Planets	Aries	Moon	v or Corrⁿ d	v or Corrⁿ d	v or Corrⁿ d
00	10° 45'.0	10° 46'.8	10° 15'.6	0.0 0.0	6.0 4.4	12.0 8.7
01	10° 45'.3	10° 47'.0	10° 15'.9	0.1 0.1	6.1 4.4	12.1 8.8
02	10° 45'.5	10° 47'.3	10° 16'.1	0.2 0.1	6.2 4.5	12.2 8.8
03	10° 45'.7	10° 47'.5	10° 16'.3	0.3 0.2	6.3 4.6	12.3 8.9
04	10° 46'.0	10° 47'.8	10° 16'.6	0.4 0.3	6.4 4.6	12.4 9.0
05	10° 46'.3	10° 48'.0	10° 16'.8	0.5 0.4	6.5 4.7	12.5 9.1
06	10° 46'.5	10° 48'.3	10° 17'.0	0.6 0.4	6.6 4.8	12.6 9.1
07	10° 46'.7	10° 48'.5	10° 17'.3	0.7 0.5	6.7 4.9	12.7 9.2
08	10° 47'.0	10° 48'.8	10° 17'.5	0.8 0.6	6.8 4.9	12.8 9.3
09	10° 47'.3	10° 49'.0	10° 17'.8	0.9 0.7	6.9 5.0	12.9 9.4
10	10° 47'.5	10° 49'.3	10° 18'.0	1.0 0.7	7.0 5.1	13.0 9.4
11	10° 47'.8	10° 49'.5	10° 18'.2	1.1 0.8	7.1 5.1	13.1 9.5
12	10° 48'.0	10° 49'.8	10° 18'.5	1.2 0.9	7.2 5.2	13.2 9.6
13	10° 48'.2	10° 50'.1	10° 18'.7	1.3 0.9	7.3 5.3	13.3 9.6
14	10° 48'.5	10° 50'.3	10° 19'.0	1.4 1.0	7.4 5.4	13.4 9.7
15	10° 48'.8	10° 50'.6	10° 19'.2	1.5 1.1	7.5 5.4	13.5 9.8
16	10° 49'.0	10° 50'.8	10° 19'.4	1.6 1.2	7.6 5.5	13.6 9.9
17	10° 49'.2	10° 51'.1	10° 19'.7	1.7 1.2	7.7 5.6	13.7 9.9
18	10° 49'.5	10° 51'.3	10° 19'.9	1.8 1.3	7.8 5.7	13.8 10.0
19	10° 49'.8	10° 51'.6	10° 20'.2	1.9 1.4	7.9 5.7	13.9 10.1
20	10° 50'.0	10° 51'.8	10° 20'.4	2.0 1.5	8.0 5.8	14.0 10.2
21	10° 50'.2	10° 52'.1	10° 20'.6	2.1 1.5	8.1 5.9	14.1 10.2
22	10° 50'.5	10° 52'.3	10° 20'.9	2.2 1.6	8.2 5.9	14.2 10.3
23	10° 50'.7	10° 52'.6	10° 21'.1	2.3 1.7	8.3 6.0	14.3 10.4
24	10° 51'.0	10° 52'.8	10° 21'.3	2.4 1.7	8.4 6.1	14.4 10.4
25	10° 51'.3	10° 53'.1	10° 21'.6	2.5 1.8	8.5 6.2	14.5 10.5
26	10° 51'.5	10° 53'.3	10° 21'.8	2.6 1.9	8.6 6.2	14.6 10.6
27	10° 51'.7	10° 53'.6	10° 22'.1	2.7 2.0	8.7 6.3	14.7 10.7
28	10° 52'.0	10° 53'.8	10° 22'.3	2.8 2.0	8.8 6.4	14.8 10.7
29	10° 52'.3	10° 54'.1	10° 22'.5	2.9 2.1	8.9 6.5	14.9 10.8
30	10° 52'.5	10° 54'.3	10° 22'.8	3.0 2.2	9.0 6.5	15.0 10.9
31	10° 52'.7	10° 54'.6	10° 23'.0	3.1 2.2	9.1 6.6	15.1 10.9
32	10° 53'.0	10° 54'.8	10° 23'.3	3.2 2.3	9.2 6.7	15.2 11.0
33	10° 53'.2	10° 55'.1	10° 23'.5	3.3 2.4	9.3 6.7	15.3 11.1
34	10° 53'.5	10° 55'.3	10° 23'.7	3.4 2.5	9.4 6.8	15.4 11.2
35	10° 53'.8	10° 55'.6	10° 24'.0	3.5 2.5	9.5 6.9	15.5 11.2
36	10° 54'.0	10° 55'.8	10° 24'.2	3.6 2.6	9.6 7.0	15.6 11.3
37	10° 54'.2	10° 56'.1	10° 24'.4	3.7 2.7	9.7 7.0	15.7 11.4
38	10° 54'.5	10° 56'.3	10° 24'.7	3.8 2.8	9.8 7.1	15.8 11.5
39	10° 54'.8	10° 56'.6	10° 24'.9	3.9 2.8	9.9 7.2	15.9 11.5
40	10° 55'.0	10° 56'.8	10° 25'.2	4.0 2.9	10.0 7.3	16.0 11.6
41	10° 55'.2	10° 57'.1	10° 25'.4	4.1 3.0	10.1 7.3	16.1 11.7
42	10° 55'.5	10° 57'.3	10° 25'.6	4.2 3.0	10.2 7.4	16.2 11.7
43	10° 55'.8	10° 57'.6	10° 25'.9	4.3 3.1	10.3 7.5	16.3 11.8
44	10° 56'.0	10° 57'.8	10° 26'.1	4.4 3.2	10.4 7.5	16.4 11.9
45	10° 56'.3	10° 58'.1	10° 26'.4	4.5 3.3	10.5 7.6	16.5 12.0
46	10° 56'.5	10° 58'.3	10° 26'.6	4.6 3.3	10.6 7.7	16.6 12.0
47	10° 56'.7	10° 58'.6	10° 26'.8	4.7 3.4	10.7 7.8	16.7 12.1
48	10° 57'.0	10° 58'.8	10° 27'.1	4.8 3.5	10.8 7.8	16.8 12.2
49	10° 57'.3	10° 59'.1	10° 27'.3	4.9 3.6	10.9 7.9	16.9 12.3
50	10° 57'.5	10° 59'.3	10° 27'.5	5.0 3.6	11.0 8.0	17.0 12.3
51	10° 57'.7	10° 59'.6	10° 27'.8	5.1 3.7	11.1 8.0	17.1 12.4
52	10° 58'.0	10° 59'.8	10° 28'.0	5.2 3.8	11.2 8.1	17.2 12.5
53	10° 58'.3	11° 00'.1	10° 28'.3	5.3 3.8	11.3 8.2	17.3 12.5
54	10° 58'.5	11° 00'.3	10° 28'.5	5.4 3.9	11.4 8.3	17.4 12.6
55	10° 58'.8	11° 00'.6	10° 28'.7	5.5 4.0	11.5 8.3	17.5 12.7
56	10° 59'.0	11° 00'.8	10° 29'.0	5.6 4.1	11.6 8.4	17.6 12.8
57	10° 59'.2	11° 01'.1	10° 29'.2	5.7 4.1	11.7 8.5	17.7 12.8
58	10° 59'.5	11° 01'.3	10° 29'.5	5.8 4.2	11.8 8.6	17.8 12.9
59	10° 59'.8	11° 01'.6	10° 29'.7	5.9 4.3	11.9 8.6	17.9 13.0
60	11° 00'.0	11° 01'.8	10° 29'.9	6.0 4.4	12.0 8.7	18.0 13.1

LATITUDE CONTRARY NAME TO DECLINATION · L.H.A. 52°, 308°

Dec.	23° Hc	d	Z	24° Hc	d	Z	25° Hc	d	Z	26° Hc	d	Z	27° Hc	d	Z	28° Hc	d	Z	29° Hc	d	Z	30° Hc	d	Z	Dec.
0	34 31.3	-28.7	107.0	34 13.5	-29.8	107.6	33 55.0	-30.8	108.3	33 35.8	-31.8	108.9	33 16.1	-32.8	109.5	32 55.7	-33.8	110.1	32 34.8	-34.8	110.7	32 13.2	-35.6	111.3	0
1	34 02.6	-29.3	108.0	33 43.7	-30.3	108.7	33 24.2	-31.4	109.3	33 04.0	-32.3	109.9	32 43.3	-33.3	110.5	32 21.9	-34.2	111.1	32 00.0	-35.1	111.7	31 37.6	-36.1	112.3	1
2	33 33.3	-29.8	109.1	33 13.4	-30.8	109.7	32 52.8	-31.8	110.3	32 31.7	-32.8	110.9	32 10.0	-33.8	111.5	31 47.7	-34.7	112.1	31 24.9	-35.6	112.7	31 01.5	-36.5	113.2	2
3	33 03.5	-30.3	110.1	32 42.6	-31.3	110.7	32 21.0	-32.3	111.3	31 58.9	-33.2	111.9	31 36.2	-34.1	112.5	31 13.0	-35.1	113.1	30 49.3	-36.0	113.6	30 25.0	-36.9	114.1	3
4	32 33.2	-30.8	111.2	32 11.3	-31.8	111.7	31 48.7	-32.7	112.3	31 25.7	-33.7	112.9	31 02.1	-34.6	113.4	30 37.9	-35.5	114.0	30 13.3	-36.4	114.5	29 48.1	-37.2	115.1	4
5	32 02.4	-31.3	112.2	31 39.5	-32.3	112.7	31 16.0	-33.2	113.3	30 52.0	-34.1	113.9	30 27.5	-35.0	114.4	30 02.4	-35.9	114.9	29 36.9	-36.8	115.4	29 10.9	-37.6	116.0	5
6	31 31.1	-31.7	113.2	31 07.2	-32.7	113.7	30 42.8	-33.6	114.3	30 17.9	-34.5	114.8	29 52.5	-35.4	115.3	29 26.5	-36.2	115.9	29 00.1	-37.1	116.4	28 33.3	-38.0	116.8	6
7	30 59.4	-32.2	114.2	30 34.5	-33.1	114.7	30 09.2	-34.0	115.2	29 43.4	-34.9	115.8	29 17.1	-35.8	116.3	28 50.3	-36.7	116.8	28 23.0	-37.4	117.3	27 55.3	-38.3	117.7	7
8	30 27.2	-32.7	115.1	30 01.4	-33.6	115.7	29 35.2	-34.5	116.2	29 08.5	-35.3	116.7	28 41.3	-36.2	117.2	28 13.6	-37.0	117.7	27 45.6	-37.8	118.1	27 17.0	-38.5	118.6	8
9	29 54.5	-33.0	116.1	29 27.9	-34.0	116.6	29 00.7	-34.8	117.1	28 33.2	-35.7	117.6	28 05.1	-36.5	118.1	27 36.6	-37.3	118.6	27 07.8	-38.2	119.0	26 38.5	-38.9	119.5	9
10	29 21.5	-33.5	117.1	28 53.9	-34.3	117.6	28 25.9	-35.2	118.1	27 57.5	-36.1	118.5	27 28.6	-36.8	119.0	26 59.3	-37.6	119.4	26 29.6	-38.4	119.9	25 59.6	-39.2	120.3	10
11	28 48.0	-33.9	118.0	28 19.6	-34.7	118.5	27 50.7	-35.5	119.0	27 21.4	-36.3	119.4	26 51.8	-37.2	119.9	26 21.7	-38.0	120.3	25 51.2	-38.7	120.7	25 20.4	-39.5	121.1	11
12	28 14.1	-34.2	119.0	27 44.9	-35.1	119.4	27 15.2	-35.9	119.9	26 45.1	-36.7	120.3	26 14.6	-37.5	120.8	25 43.7	-38.2	121.2	25 12.5	-39.0	121.6	24 40.9	-39.8	122.0	12
13	27 39.9	-34.6	119.9	27 09.8	-35.5	120.3	26 39.3	-36.3	120.8	26 08.4	-37.1	121.2	25 37.1	-37.8	121.6	25 05.5	-38.6	122.0	24 33.5	-39.3	122.4	24 01.1	-40.0	122.8	13
14	27 05.3	-35.0	120.8	26 34.3	-35.7	121.3	26 03.0	-36.5	121.7	25 31.3	-37.3	122.1	24 59.3	-38.1	122.5	24 26.9	-38.8	122.9	23 54.2	-39.6	123.2	23 21.1	-40.2	123.6	14
15	26 30.3	-35.3	121.7	25 58.6	-36.1	122.1	25 26.5	-36.9	122.6	24 54.0	-37.6	122.9	24 21.2	-38.4	123.3	23 48.1	-39.1	123.7	23 14.6	-39.8	124.1	22 40.9	-40.5	124.4	15
16	25 55.0	-35.8	122.6	25 22.5	-36.4	123.0	24 49.6	-37.2	123.4	24 16.4	-37.9	123.8	23 42.8	-38.6	124.2	23 09.0	-39.4	124.5	22 34.8	-40.0	124.9	22 00.4	-40.8	125.2	16
17	25 19.4	-36.0	123.5	24 46.1	-36.8	123.9	24 12.4	-37.4	124.3	23 38.5	-38.2	124.7	23 04.2	-38.9	125.0	22 29.6	-39.6	125.4	21 54.8	-40.3	125.7	21 19.6	-40.9	126.0	17
18	24 43.4	-36.3	124.4	24 09.3	-37.0	124.8	23 35.0	-37.8	125.1	23 00.3	-38.5	125.5	22 25.3	-39.2	125.8	21 50.0	-39.8	126.2	21 14.5	-40.5	126.5	20 38.7	-41.2	126.8	18
19	24 07.1	-36.5	125.3	23 32.3	-37.3	125.6	22 57.2	-38.0	126.0	22 21.8	-38.7	126.3	21 46.1	-39.3	126.7	21 10.2	-40.1	127.0	20 34.0	-40.7	127.3	19 57.5	-41.3	127.6	19
20	23 30.6	-36.9	126.1	22 55.0	-37.5	126.5	22 19.2	-38.2	126.8	21 43.1	-38.9	127.1	21 06.8	-39.7	127.5	20 30.1	-40.2	127.8	19 53.3	-40.9	128.1	19 16.2	-41.6	128.3	20
21	22 53.7	-37.1	127.0	22 17.5	-37.8	127.3	21 41.0	-38.4	127.7	21 04.2	-39.2	128.0	20 27.1	-39.8	128.3	19 49.9	-40.5	128.6	19 12.4	-41.2	128.8	18 34.6	-41.7	129.1	21
22	22 16.6	-37.4	127.9	21 39.7	-38.1	128.2	21 02.5	-38.8	128.5	20 25.0	-39.4	128.8	19 47.3	-40.0	129.1	19 09.4	-40.7	129.3	18 31.2	-41.3	129.6	17 52.9	-41.9	129.9	22
23	21 39.2	-37.6	128.7	21 01.6	-38.3	129.0	20 23.7	-39.0	129.3	19 45.6	-39.6	129.6	19 07.3	-40.3	129.9	18 28.7	-40.9	130.1	17 49.9	-41.4	130.4	17 11.0	-42.1	130.6	23
24	21 01.6	-37.9	129.5	20 23.3	-38.6	129.8	19 44.7	-39.1	130.1	19 06.0	-39.8	130.4	18 27.0	-40.4	130.6	17 47.8	-41.0	130.9	17 08.5	-41.7	131.1	16 28.9	-42.2	131.3	24
25	20 23.7	-38.1	130.4	19 44.7	-38.7	130.6	19 05.6	-39.4	130.9	18 26.2	-40.1	131.2	17 46.6	-40.7	131.4	17 06.8	-41.2	131.6	16 26.8	-41.8	131.9	15 46.7	-42.4	132.1	25
26	19 45.6	-38.3	131.2	19 06.0	-39.0	131.5	18 26.2	-39.6	131.7	17 46.1	-40.2	131.9	17 05.9	-40.8	132.2	16 25.6	-41.4	132.4	15 45.0	-41.9	132.6	15 04.3	-42.5	132.8	26
27	19 07.3	-38.6	132.0	18 27.0	-39.2	132.3	17 46.6	-39.8	132.5	17 05.9	-40.4	132.7	16 25.1	-40.9	132.9	15 44.2	-41.5	133.2	15 03.1	-42.1	133.4	14 21.8	-42.6	133.5	27
28	18 28.7	-38.8	132.8	17 47.8	-39.3	133.1	17 06.8	-40.0	133.3	16 25.6	-40.6	133.5	15 44.2	-41.1	133.7	15 02.7	-41.7	133.9	14 21.0	-42.3	134.1	13 39.2	-42.8	134.3	28
29	17 49.9	-38.9	133.6	17 08.5	-39.6	133.8	16 26.8	-40.1	134.1	15 45.0	-40.7	134.3	15 03.1	-41.3	134.5	14 21.0	-41.8	134.7	13 38.7	-42.3	134.8	12 56.4	-42.9	135.0	29

Excerpt from H.O. 229 Latitude 15-30

APPENDIX 5: GREAT CIRCLE SAILING EXAMPLE

Departing Jacksonville, Fl.: Lat 30° - 20.1'N, Long. 080° - 56.2' W
Arriving: Brest, France: Lat. 48° - 14.0 N, 005° – 05.4'

DLO=   080° - 56.2'
      -005° - 05.4'
        75° - 50.8'

1. Calculate Distance along the track:

Cos D=   (Sin L1 x Sin L2)
         + (Cos L1 x Cos L2 x Cos Dlo)
Cos D=   (Sin 30.33 x Sin 48.23)
         + (Cos 30.33 X Cos 48.23 x Cos 75.85)
Cos D=   .51718
Distance=   3,531 NM

2. Calculate Initial Course

Tan C= $\dfrac{\text{Sin Dlo}}{(\text{Cos L1} \times \text{Tan L2}) - (\text{Sin L1} \times \text{Cos Dlo})}$

Tan C= $\dfrac{\text{Sin 75.85}}{(\text{Cos 30.33} \times \text{Tan 48.23}) - (\text{Sin 30.33} \times \text{Cos 75.85})}$

Tan C= 1.15034 = 49°

Course Angle= N 49 E, Initial Course is 49°

Latitude of the Vertex

3. Calculate the Latitude and Longitude of the vertex

Cos Lv=   Cos L1 x Sin C
Cos Lv=   Cos 30.33 x Sin 49.0
Cos Lv=   .651412

Latitude of the Vertex= 49. 35° or 49° - 21'

Longitude of the Vertex

Dlov is the Distance from the starting latitude (L1) to the vertex in degrees

Sin Dlov=   Cos C / Sin Lv
Sin Dlov=   Cos 49/ Sin 49.35= .86470
Dlov=   59.848° or 59°- 51'

Long. of
the Vertex

080° - 56.2' W
-059° - 51.0' W   (subtract because we are going east)
021° - 05.2' W

Latitude of the Vertex= 49° - 21' N (49.35°)
Longitude of the Vertex= 021 °– 05.2' W

4. Finding points along the track.

In this example points along the track, or waypoints along the Great Circle route, are calculating every ten degrees from the vertex.
  Dlovx is the difference of longitude from the vertex to point x.

Tan Lx=   Cos Dlovx x Tan Lv

Descr	Tan Lx	Lat of Waypoint
A- 031 °– 05.2' W (10° west of vertex) Tan Lx= Cos 10°x Tan 49.35°	1.14697	48.92 ° or 48° - 55.2'
B- 041 °– 05.2' W (20° west of vertex) Tan Lx= Cos 20°x Tan 49.35°	1.09442	47.58° or 48° - 34.8'
C- 051 °– 05.2' W (30° west of vertex) Tan Lx= Cos 30°x Tan 49.35°	1.0086	45.25° or 45° - 15.0'
D- 061 °– 05.2' W (40° west of vertex) Tan Lx= Cos 40°x Tan 49.35°	0.89218	41. 74° or 41° - 44.0'
E- 071 °– 05.2' W (50° west of vertex) Tan Lx= Cos 50°x Tan 49.35°	0.74863	36.82° or 36° - 49.2'

Great Circle Voyage Track

Way Points on Great Circle	Latitude	Longitude	True Course to next WP	Distance
WP0	36° - 49.2'	071 ° - 05.2'	057.7°	551
WP1	41° - 44.0'	061 ° - 05.2'	064.2°	484.9
WP2	45° - 15.0'	051 ° - 05.2'	071.4°	438
WP3	47° - 34.8'	041 ° - 05.2'	079.1°	409
WP4	48° - 55.2'	031 ° - 05.2'	085.8°	395
WP5	49° - 21'	021 ° - 05.2'	093.7°	395
WP6	48° - 55.2'	011 ° - 05.		

Once the waypoints are established, distance and course to steer between them is a rhumb line and may be calculated either by Mercator sailing or by entering the waypoints on an ECDIS.

APPENDIX 6: NAVIGATION FORMULAS

Speed

Time= Distance(nm) / Speed (nm per hr.)

Distance= Speed (nm per hr.) x Time (hr.)

▶ **The Sailings: Mercator**

To find course and distance to a destination when given departure and arrival latitude and longitude use the following formula:

Tan C = DLO/DM   D = Dlat/Cos C

To find new Latitude and Longitude when given departure Lat/long and Course and Distance use the following formula:

Dlat = Cos C x D   Dlo = DM x Tan C

Mid-Latitude

P=   Dlo x Cos Lm

TanC=   P/DL

D=   DLat/Cos C

▶ **Parallel Sailing**

P = DLO x Cos Lat

Where

Lm = the middle latitude between departure and arrival. If departure is 20° and arrival is 10° than the Lm is 15°.

DM=   Difference of Meridional Parts

DL=   the Difference of Latitude
        between departure and arrival

Dlo=   difference of longitude

P=   departure in nautical miles

C=   course angle

▶ **Great Circle Sailings Formulas:**
Initial Course and Distance-

$$\text{Cos D} = (\text{Sin L1} \times \text{Sin L2*}) + (\text{Cos L1} \times \text{Cos L2} \times \text{Cos Dlo})$$

$$\text{Tan C} = \frac{\text{Sin Dlo}}{(\text{Cos L1} \times \text{Tan L2*}) - (\text{Sin L1} \times \text{Cos Dlo})}$$

* negative when crossing the equator

Finding the Latitude and Longitude of the Vertex

Lat of the vertex-   Cos Lv= Cos L1 x Sin C

Long of the vertex- Sin Dlov= $\dfrac{\text{Cos C}}{\text{Sin Lv}}$

Note

- **C** is the Course angle, not the true course

   Dlov is the difference of longitude between the point of departure and the vertex. This is added or subtracted depending on direction of travel

   Distance from the point of Departure to the Vertex-

$$\text{Sin Dv} = \text{Cos L1 x Sin Dlov}$$

Finding points along the Great Circle Track (X)

The Latitude of a point X along the Great Circle Track:

$$\text{Tan Lx} = \text{Cos Dlovx x Tan Lv}$$

or

$$\text{Sin Lx} = \text{Sin Lv x Cos Dvx}$$

Compass Correction
Azimuth

$$\text{Tan Z} = \frac{\cos D \text{ x } \sin LHA}{(\cos L \sin D) - (\sin L \cos D \cos LHA)}$$

Where D= declination

L= latitude

LHA= Local Hour Angle

1. If LHA is greater than 180 than subtract answer from 180.

2. If Latitude and declination are contrary (i.e., North latitude and South Declination) then Sin d, in the denominator, is negative

Amplitude

$$\text{Sin Amplitude} = \frac{\text{Sin Declination}}{\text{Cos Latitude}}$$

Prefix is East for rising, West setting

Suffix is North for north declination and South for south declination

Magnetic Compass

To find the True heading from Magnetic Compass Heading (PSC)

Compass +/- Deviation = Magnetic Heading
+/- Variation = True Heading

Compass Heading to True Heading, Add West/ Subtract East

True Heading to Compass Heading, Add East/ Subtract West

Celestial Formula:

Local Hour Angle:
LHA= GHA + East Long.
LHA= GHA – West Long.

GHA of a Star

GHA Star = GHA Aires + SHA Star

Computed Altitude (Hc)

$$\text{Sin H} = \text{Sin L Sin D} + \text{Cos L Cos D Cos LHA}$$

Where

H=   **Hc**
L=   **Latitude of assumed position**
D=   **declination of the body at the time of the sight**
LHA= **Local Hour Angle**
           of the body at the time of the sight

APPENDIX 7: NAVIGATIONAL FORMULAS FROM THE U.S. GOVERNMENT

- National Oceanic and Atmospheric Administration (NOAA)
- Tide Predictions: http://tidesandcurrents.noaa.gov/tide_predictions.shtml
- Tidal Current Predictions: http://tidesandcurrents.noaa.gov/curr_pred.html
- Marine Weather Forecast: http://www.nws.noaa.gov/om/marine/home.htm
- National Geospatil Intelligence Agency (NGA)
- The NGA publishes a wealth of voyage planning information on their website Nautical Publications
- The link below allows downloads for all of the following: http://msi.nga.mil/NGAPortal/MSI.portal?_nfpb=true&_pageLabel=msi_portal_page_62
- American Practical Navigator- Bowditch
- Atlas of Pilot Charts
- Chart No. 1
- Distances Between Ports
- International Code of Signals
- NGA List of Lights
- Radar Navigation and Maneuvering Board Manual
- Radio navigational Aids
- Sailing Directions Enroute
- Sailing Directions Planning Guide
- Sight Reduction Tables for Marine Navigation (HO 229)
- USCG Light List